FRAMED BY OUR HOUSES

Sunny, Rainy and Snowy Sketches of Canadian Living

William R. Marshall

www.framedbyourhouses.ca
Use this to see the house pictures,
and where and how to buy the book.

 FriesenPress

One Printers Way
Altona, MB R0G 0B0
Canada

www.friesenpress.com

Copyright © 2025 by William R. Marshall
First Edition — 2025

All rights reserved.

No part of this publication may be reproduced in any form, or by any means, electronic or mechanical, including photocopying, recording, or any information browsing, storage, or retrieval system, without permission in writing from FriesenPress.

ISBN
978-1-03-835533-1 (Hardcover)
978-1-03-835532-4 (Paperback)
978-1-03-835534-8 (eBook)

1. BIOGRAPHY & AUTOBIOGRAPHY, PERSONAL MEMOIRS

Distributed to the trade by The Ingram Book Company

CONTENTS

Prologue 1
Chapter 1: Trading Roots for Webs 5
Chapter 2: Magnetic Fields 11
Chapter 3: Wave Action 21
Chapter 4: Grandparents' Houses 31
Chapter 5: Gateway to Adulthood 35
Chapter 6: New Worlds, New Friends 49
Chapter 7: Small Window Frames 57
Chapter 8: The Charms of Country Living 61
Chapter 9: A Student's Life 67
Chapter 10: Living Together 71
Chapter 11: The End of the Road 75
Chapter 12: Retreats 89
Chapter 13: The Golden Rule 91
Chapter 14: Longhouses, Short Memories 103
Chapter 15: Prairie Houses 109
Chapter 16: Maritime Wilderness 115
Chapter 17: Townhomes and Community 129
Chapter 18: Living in the Suburbs, Again 137
Chapter 19: The Fabric House 145
Chapter 20: The Last House Chapter 163
Chapter 21: Trailer Life 169
Chapter 22: My Friends' Houses 175
Epilogue 189
Where The Author Has Lived 197

PROLOGUE

I live the Chinese curse of *may you have an interesting life*. To the Chinese, who revere order and tradition, this implies that something or someplace new is always just around the corner. I realize that some people live in only one or a few houses and in the same city or town throughout their entire lives. That is normal, or at least it used to be. I've read that four hundred years ago, the average person lived within eight kilometres of where they were born and didn't travel more than sixty kilometres from home in their lifetime. Truly indigenous people, like most American First Nations people, have lived in the same small region for five hundred generations.

Like some other people, however, I have lived in thirty-two places that I can remember something about. That covers about eighteen cities or areas and three provinces—Ontario, Quebec, and British Columbia. I have spent varying lengths of time in houses in the Maritimes, on the prairies, and in the western Arctic. In my tent, my fabric house, and in our travel trailer, I have visited a great many more places across our great land. I have had a wonderful life. The Chinese curse has an upside, too.

Why would I bother telling you about the houses I have lived in?

In its own smallish way, a house is like a world, a micro-culture central to the life in and around it. Its size defines how many people are apt to live in it and the differing social dynamics between, say, an older couple living in a small house or eight unrelated students living in a big house.

The location helps define who can live there—on a quiet city street or kilometres from nowhere—and survive the experience. A unique culture surrounds each house, from the local neighbours and neighbourhood to the economic, language, religious, ethnic, and social roots of the region. It may be a French-Canadian farmhouse, or an English-Canadian one, a cabin in the bush, a native longhouse or prairie house. Every house I have lived in or visited a while has left an imprint of some kind on me. The houses in your life have done the same to you. A part of your Canadian identity is carved into you from that experience.

Maybe this book will help those who have a fear of moving. Moving is a leap into the unknown. Perhaps reading my experiences will prepare you a little.

Perhaps you have not enjoyed living where you do and you are looking for something better, but you are not sure what the *something* is that you are looking for. You will find in this book a host of different types of living, different ways of living with neighbours or without them. You will find descriptions of good places to bring up your children, and a few not-so-good ones. If you are looking for community, you will see how to find it—or how to find isolation, if that is your bent.

For those of you who do not move around very much, the stories may give you some insight into what it means to be a "highly mobile" or "cosmopolitan" North American, the pluses and the minuses. You might find a deeper understanding of the strengths you have in enduring, in being indigenous to one place, one building, for a long time. Rooted.

On the other hand, if you have moved around a fair bit, you may find lots of "ah-hah" and "been there, done that" parts. You may be part of the new generation that is developing webs instead of roots.

Or, you can see the stories as a travelogue about many parts of Canada and several of its distinct cultures—to prove Canadians are not boring and to get a glimpse into their lives as proof. In this vast and heterogeneous land, its different communities are more like the deli section at the supermarket. Every item looks different, smells and tastes unique. Some are appealing, some not, depending on your taste.

Canada has so many lifestyles in it that you cannot imagine them all. I can tell you about a few dozen of them, a pretty varied selection, but there are hundreds more. Although this book covers a period of time from the middle 1950s to 2025, the lifestyles described in it are more or less timeless. You will find people somewhere in Canada still living the older ones I write about. Even the stories of new immigrants settling in today in our major cities are most likely repeats of stories that happened time and again in our history.

In this book, parents will also see how where you live has an effect on your children. Who and what they can be is often proscribed by where they grow up.

These stories will help you remember the places you have lived and take another look at how houses have framed your life.

CHAPTER ONE

Trading Roots for Webs

The idea of writing about what houses have taught me came to me a few days after my father's funeral in London, Ontario, in 1995. Although my parents had moved around a fair bit, they retired in the city they grew up in. Many of the people who came to the funeral had known my parents their entire lives, and some had parents who knew their parents, and even their parents. My dad was a member of a lodge and he was a third-generation member of it. Current members came to perform their own service at the departing of a member. Such are the roots of some people.

My own roots do not go very deep in any one place. I have traded in my roots for webs.

I guess it was the contrast between my own cross-country wanderings and my parents' stability that got me thinking. For five years, I ran a drop-in centre called a Family Place in a suburb of Vancouver, British Columbia. It is rare to find a "local" who has lived more than forty years in one suburb. When you are not surrounded by your physical history and your kinfolk, you lose touch with who you are, with your family's wisdom, and with reference points and familiar landmarks.

In Canada, almost everyone is a relative newcomer, and not many of us have close family nearby. A Family Place tries to provide new parents a sense of community, a play-space for their children, a parenting and marital resource, and many other of the things that extended families living in one place used to provide for young families. Mobility stretches your blood too thin. We are trying to build webs of friendships and relationships where once we had family ties and roots.

Visiting my mother's ancestral home in London a few days after my father's funeral, I saw some of the roots side of life that I seldom see in western Canada. It is a younger place.

What I felt on entering that old homestead was akin to time travel. Something about the smells, the light in the room, the pictures, the creaks in the floor, brought back childhood memories—and I was ten years old again. As if from habit, I had to look around for certain things that I wanted to see again. The old, small and crowded kitchen hadn't changed. Its ceiling was barely two metres high, and cupboards covered all the walls except for the door and three windows.

I remembered spending a lot of time there almost seventy years ago. In a way, it was strange that these rooms had not changed, though I had. I got to thinking about what it would be like to live in one house all my life, where my parents and their parents grew up and with the same decor for two generations, at least. And after mulling that over for several weeks, I began to see houses in a new way.

The first story in the book describes this recent encounter with my past. Then, the stories leap back forty-five years and progress to the present, mostly. I tried to keep to the truth, but after many years, there may be some flaws in my recollection of details and maybe a few "stretchers," as Huck Finn would say. But mostly, it's the truth.

Sometimes I try to cover up people's identities, just to be kind and keep out of trouble. There is no beginning and no end, really. There's no plot, or sex (well, maybe a little), and no reason to finish the book before you go to sleep. So, you can read the stories in any order you like and not really miss anything.

I have an ancestral home in London, Ontario on Saunby Street. A day after my father's funeral, my mother, brothers and I went out to visit some old relatives who were too immobile to come to the funeral. The old Stevens' homestead we visited was a house of history, including a bit of my own and my next younger brother Gary's. Sort of by accident, my parents bought a house in the same London neighbourhood when I was about seven years-old—around 1954. We lived there until I was twelve. Only a short block and a turn away was the old grey house of my mother's ancestors.

I soon learned that it was a good bet for milk and cookies in winter and for cherries, pears, peaches, and apples in summer. Out back was a long chicken coop I climbed up on to get the best cherries. My "Uncle" John and his sister, Ruth, lived there, and sometimes another widowed sister for a decade or two. John was very handsome, very shy, and very quiet. He was a milkman his entire working life.

Quite a few times on Saturday mornings, John would let me help him on his milk run. We'd start by grooming and hitching the horse, checking for the shovel and bucket on the back of wagon, then proceed up to the dairy to load the milk. This was a thoroughly modern dairy that had just installed cardboard milk carton machines. I got to fill up the waxer pots, load up the flattened milk cartons, and push the fist-sized green START button. The automated process of popping open, waxing and filling the milk cartons as they wound their way up and down lanes and chutes, was a tribute to Rube Goldberg. I remember the smell of the place to this day.

The dairy and the old house were linked by the mystery of having more rooms than I ever got to see inside. There were doors down dark halls or cellars that I just didn't open!

The original five-by-ten-metre, two-storey house was built sometime in the 1850s or 1860s by a great-great-grandfather and his brothers on my mother's side. At least that's what we think. Job Stevens was indentured to the merchant navy, and we have his signed release form, dated 1851. He had worked his way to Canada, only to learn that his young wife had died the year before back in England.

The house had been lived in by descendants ever since, the last of whom was my "Aunt" Ruth. Covered in a dark grey stucco which sagged and bulged in many places, the old homestead tilted and bent in different directions on each corner. The front, heavy-walled balcony sagged in the middle, about thirty centimetres off-line. The house's occupant suffered similar effects. Then eighty-five and getting feeble—in body only—Ruth lived alone and was the keeper of her side of the family history. Single all her life like brother John, she kindly cared for and buried all her closest relatives.

The small front parlour room had a staircase to the right leading to the second floor. Made of dark oak and far heavier than necessary, the stairs creaked and squealed with each step. Once at the top, there was a large sitting room that served as a hall for two very small bedrooms. Each held one old size double bed, a one-drawer-wide chest of drawers, plus an itty-bitty closet.

There were four chairs arranged in the sitting room, sort of facing each other. A spindle rocker with crocheted seat and back cushions. Two floral stuffed chairs with critter feet and a dark wooden chair. Propped in the seat of each one was a large, framed black-and-white photograph of one of our ancestors. The older ones had men with foot-long beards and women covered from head to toe in cloth. The newer ones had shorter beards and less clothing. Trying not to disturb their conversation, I had slipped by them to peer into the bedrooms. The beds were all made up, but the rooms were bereft of personal affects or wall art. Only more photos of yet more ancestors propped on each pillow. I couldn't tell you who they all were, but it's a sure bet they all lived in that house at one time. Still did.

Among the ancestors were a wife and daughter drowned in a freak ferry accident in the 1880s—a Victoria Day fireworks cruise on the Thames River (Ontario) when everyone came to one side of the ferry to see the show. The Stevens husband dived for and saved many, dragged many more dead bodies ashore, all the while hoping to find his own family. Someone else did. Other cousins also died that night. Others died in the world wars.

The last tragedy had to do with Ruth. Her older sisters had married and had not borne children. This was not a good thing ninety years ago. Ruth, the youngest, never had a serious date or relationship because of the "curse of barrenness" on the family. Of course, it could easily have been the men the sisters married who were infertile, but that was not usually where the fingers pointed. Who knows?

And so ended the living history of the Stevens' homestead. There being no offspring of those left inheriting and inhabiting the house, the house fell from family hands. When Ruth died, I thought that the house would probably have to be buried, too. It had stood for some 140 years at that time and hadn't been remodelled since the turn of the century.

In our own family's search for roots, the furthest back we get is on another branch on my mother's side, the Hustons, where we have found the ancestral castle in southern Scotland dating to the early 1400s. Since arriving in Canada some 170 years ago, none of us has returned to it. We built new ancestral homes here.

Canada is a land of immigrants, some of whom arrived over three hundred years ago in Acadia and Quebec while others just arrived yesterday. Now, most of us are in-betweeners. Having an ancestral home in Canada means that you have some roots here rather than somewhere else. It makes you Canadian, though not as indigenous as First Nations people are to this land. New Canadians can often be truly Canadian, too, though that is not always so. Some come here with the intention of becoming Canadian in every way they can, and they often participate more in our cultural and national life than many old-time Canadians do. Some come here merely out of convenience for their businesses or careers, or to escape a land they no longer want to call home because of its political situation. Maybe that is an explanation many old-timers would find in their family history, too. Why did they come here?

Up until a few generations ago, most immigrants spread themselves across the land rather evenly. Needing only brawn and resourcefulness, they could settle anywhere there were jobs or farmland. Now, most newcomers come to Canada's largest cities and rarely venture into our heartlands and more remote areas. It is a different time, and we are still trying to understand it.

Ancestral homes may be disappearing from our lives as well. People move about so much, especially within big cities, that it may soon be rare to find anyone who has one. How do you find your roots when that occurs? I've read that the average North American moves eleven times in their life. Where are you from?

I found in my own search to answer those questions that I had not a single root, but a web of life in Canada. Perhaps that is what lies ahead for most of us.

CHAPTER TWO

Magnetic Fields

Beaufort Street, London, Ontario

You do so much important stuff in your first three years. Like learning to walk and talk and play and wearing your last poopy diaper. You think you'd remember something. Why it is that you can't remember anything important you did before you were three? My mother told me that the first house I lived in, from birth to age three or so, was on Whetter Avenue. I do not remember a thing about it.

For a short while, my parents rented an upstairs apartment on Duchess Avenue, the only recollection I have of it being some very scary open stairs on the outside of the building. To this day, I do not like such stairs.

The first house I actually remember living in was in a newer area of north London, near the University of Western Ontario and just a block north of the Stevens' homestead. It was a newly built house, small and square and white. I could crawl through the milk box.

Remember those? A small cubby with a little door on the outside and another on the inside, just big enough for an elf.

The house faced a ragged field that led to the Thames River and dense woods along the banks. In the summertime, a bridge made of barrels would be wired across the river to give our neighbourhood access to Gibbons Park and its swimming pool on the other side. A big tree hung over the bank with a tempting swinging rope on it. Every kid needs one of those.

My father finished the painting in the house and then built a recreation room in the basement. It was a wonderful place. It was painted black, everywhere, and we cut out potatoes with designs on them and dabbed bright fluorescent colours all over the floor and walls. Handprints, too. Tiny star-lights on the ceiling. An obligatory bar in the back and a plastic garden thing at the other end. Quite a sight, I'm sure, but it was in back then.

For me and my friends, the rec room was the command centre of our space station. Foil-covered cardboard boxes were our space and robot suits. TV rabbit ears, our antennae. A Morse code practice pad with a flashing light and click or buzz sound choices was our communications centre.

Having convinced all the families on the block to buy the same gauge of model railway, our rec room also became Treasure Island—with a massive railway system, of course. Once we had assembled every kid's tracks and trains and transformers, added the smoke drops to the engines' stacks, dimmed the lights, and cranked up the trains… we were transported to Never Never Land. One train started in the low beach area and rose up over the sofa (the highlands), through the curtains and up to the furnace and hot water heater (the mountaintop, the Indigenous village) then down to the laundry tubs and over the tool bench (the heartless city of adults) and on to the plastic garden, and back to the lowlands by the sea—and Captain Hook.

By the time I was eleven or so, my mom had repainted the floor and added those footprint silhouettes for all the dance steps. She would teach me and my friends how to dance. We even had a few sock hops there, with real girls, too. That's what happens when you outgrow your train set, I guess.

My father built a rec room in every house we owned after that. The way my parents used the rec room was quite different, however. Cocktail parties before going out to other parties were all the rage. Our parents dressed up in some very fancy finery. The women were painted with makeup and smelling like I don't know what. Men wore black suits and fancy shirts with cufflinks and studded buttons and unusually bright ties. Not work ties.

The women mostly stayed upstairs in the living room and the men ended up in the basement, around the bar, talking their kind of talk. Eventually they would all be upstairs, still talking away and getting ready to head on to the next party. One of my earliest and only memories of the upstairs of the Beaufort Street house was sitting on my father's lap, in my jammies, with my ear pressed to his chest and listening to the deep murmuring sounds of his voice. This inevitably put me right to sleep.

The picture window looked out on a football-sized field—or rather, the field looked in the window. It called out, "Come. Come visit me. Play in the grasses. Catch the grasshoppers. Sneak up on the butterflies. Run to the forest at the back of the field. Swing on the willows, young Tarzan. Make it to the river beyond, young Huck." So the house was just a place to stay between the times you were in the field. I'm pretty sure that all houses with fields in the front would be like that.

My field was city-owned, untended and a scrubby mix of grass and clover, burrs, and Queen Anne's Lace, bright purple thistles and milkweed plants with monarch butterflies and their gloriously fat, green caterpillars. In the fall, the city dump trucks would pile a mountain of leaves for us to play in. Approaching the river, a tall forest of willows, oaks, and maple trees shaded and cooled the riverbank. Thickets of stinging nettles and berry bushes crowded the forest edges.

When I was younger, I could only go partway into the field. The first part was a little hill—just fun enough for a saucer ride in the winter snows or for creating rushing rivers among the Dinky Toy towns we had built on hot summer days. When I reached the age of the middle of the field, through the tall grasses I did chase grasshoppers and snakes, butterflies and wild boar and elephants and lions and…

I also had a wonderful dog at the time. Cindy, a brown and white springer spaniel, was ready to play any game you wanted, or be any creature you needed. She was also really good at keeping you out of trouble. If Cindy got wet, Mom would know we had been to the river. If she was covered in burrs, Mom would know we had been down near or into the forest. The tell-tail dog.

By the time I was ten, I could go to the forest and the river with my friends—sometimes by myself, too. The Thames was fairly wide in places, maybe thirty metres, and relatively calm, but it narrowed to half that in other places, and rapids ran. Large, light-coloured stones and gravel stretched as far as the eye could see in either direction. Only in a few places was the water deep enough to hide the stony bottom. Bright, long strips of gravel bars and mini islands appeared around every bend.

On my side, the forest came right to the river's edge. On the opposite bank was Gibbons Park, with open fields of grass and only a few large trees dotted here and there. Cicadas screamed overhead on hot days, giant dragon flies patrolled the riverbanks, and squawky kingfishers swooped back and forth. In the evening, it would be strings of little brown bats performing acrobatic tricks over the river while fireflies winked on and off everywhere. A jar full of fireflies by your bed is like sleeping with fairies.

We played "cowboys and Indians," mostly. Sneaking up on each other through the bushes. Then, "Kapow! You're dead." I don't know why it was so much fun, but it was.

After seeing *The Adventures of Huckleberry Finn*, my friend Roy and I built our own rafts and poled our way up the Thames River to the university stadium to gather pop bottles for the refund. The river was wide, shallow, and calm on the way up. We never seemed to account for the extra weight of the pop bottles when we built the raft. Also, to trade in the bottles, we had to go farther downstream to a store near the river, and through some fun rapids on the way. We had to walk behind the raft and keep it from tipping or sinking.

Along the way, we would catch big crayfish and boil them up in an old tin can on the beach. Crayfish tails are close to lobster, if you imagine the taste just right. Cindy couldn't catch the crayfish, but she did have a knack for cornering and catching suckers and carp in the shallows. She would flip them onto the rocks and play with their flipping about until they quit moving, which was when we could move in to pick them up for a quick meal. God only knows how polluted and worm-ridden those fish were (as my parents pointed out), but we boys never seemed to notice. Fire-roasted fish on a stick seemed like pretty fine fare to us. Probably, luckily, we cooked the heck out of those worms.

I came to know the river very well, its seasonal moods and all the critters that lived in it. I had an aquarium with samples of everything I could find and catch—water striders, water boatmen, crayfish, stickle-backs, darters, minnows, even a water scorpion, the king of the bugs. My tank held many nymphs, freshwater shrimp, and other life until I put the water scorpion in. Within days, most of the other critters had disappeared. A water scorpion is similar to a praying mantis, and just as voracious.

From the river's snapping turtles, I also learned that home is where the food is. I found some plate-sized snapping turtles playing around in the sand near the river's edge. (They were laying eggs, but I hadn't noticed that.) So, I decided to take a couple of them home with me. For over a hundred yards, I carried two huge snapping turtles, each by the prehistoric, spiked tail, their pink mouths open to chomp on my skinny shins at any time. Once on the front lawn, in the kiddie swimming pool, they seemed quite content to eat the wieners and raw hamburger we fed them. Soon, they had stopped their hissing and snapping and merely withdrew their heads if we got too near. They were still there in the morning.

My parents had had enough of them by mid-day, and so I was instructed to take them back just the way I had brought them up from the river. I did put them right back where I found them and said goodbye.

By suppertime, the two turtles had made their way back to our front lawn, where they waited patiently. Deciding not to feed them this time, I took them back to the river again, farther downstream. Then there was the pet bat, the pet rabbit, the pet snakes and toads, and soon there was little distinction between the river and my bedroom. I think I was lucky that Nintendo and computer games hadn't been invented yet.

A river is not always peaceful. I remember seeing the barrel bridge being torn apart in a sudden flood. Huge curls of water twisted it and snapped its wires. One winter, I fell through the ice near a lead in the middle. I went right under the ice and popped up in the lead. By the time I made it home, my snowsuit was frozen stiff and clinking as I staggered like a robot up to our front door. Do you know what mothers do to you when they find you all frozen up like that? I don't remember what happened after I got home. But I didn't go near the frozen river again.

Hunting was something that almost every boy wanted to try. Frogs, squirrels, rabbits, partridge, and other prey successfully eluded me 99 percent of the time. For my eleventh birthday (in November), I had been given a new bow-and-arrow set. I got pretty good at target practice and decided to go hunting down in the forest. As a boy, you learned not to first ask if you could do such things.

My trusty hound, Cindy, was busy flushing rabbits and birds out of the underbrush, all of which ran or flew off far out of distance of a boy's bow and arrow. Then, almost beside me, Cindy leaped, and the thunder pounded—a ring-necked pheasant sprang up a few yards away, wings banging loudly, like my little heart, and I up and shot my arrow at it. It dropped out of sight and made no noise. To my utter amazement, I had killed it outright with a perfect shot.

I could not believe that I had done it. And the poor bird looked so spectacularly beautiful—a regal male pheasant with golden green neck feathers, a bright white ring around its neck, other feathers that glistened and sparkled and enormously long tail feathers. My mind raced with conflicting visions of myself. The great hunter. Wonderful feathers for my Indigenous headdress. Saying we'll dine like royalty on a fine pheasant. How could I have killed such a beautiful creature? What would my parents say?

As I came marching across the field toward our house, my bow and arrows and a pheasant slung over my shoulder, my trusty dog at my side, my mother caught sight of me from the front window. She ran out and hustled me quickly into the house. I could tell that she was absolutely amazed at my bagging a pheasant, and she threw it in a plastic bag and into the freezer before I could even tell her what happened. I then learned that hunting was not permitted in the city. I also learned that pheasants were out of season. I learned that there might be big fines if anyone heard that I had shot a pheasant, so I couldn't even tell my friends. It was a long lecture.

As a family, we watched the first TV shows in our living room. *Ed Sullivan, Bonanza, Howdy Doody, Maggie Muggins, Father Knows Best, Leave It to Beaver, American Bandstand, I Love Lucy, The Honeymooners, The Wonderful World of Disney, Hockey Night in Canada.* You could talk with anybody about the TV shows you had seen, because everyone had seen the same shows. There was only one channel.

I mentioned earlier that Beaufort Street was near the university. My grandfather had a few acquaintances up there and he took me there several times, each visit memorable to this day. At our summer cottage, I had discovered what I thought were extraordinarily rare and wonderful stones. At Kettle Point, on Lake Ontario, there was a shale bank where these stones formed. In each kettle (a semi-round hole in the shale) you found a perfectly round stone or boulder—some a few centimetres in diameter and others a metre or more across. The smaller ones weighed three times what you would expect a stone to weigh, and if you broke it open, it glimmered with crystals. I had a cigar box collection of them.

My grandfather took me to the geology department at the University of Western Ontario to see if we could find out what the stones were. After being introduced to a grey-haired professor, I simply plunked my stones down on the professor's desk and asked if he knew what they were.

He studied them for a short while and then said, "These are magnetites. You must have found them at Kettle Point."

I was dumbfounded. How could someone know so much that they could just look at a stone and tell you where you found it? The professor then showed me the rows of glass cases with myriad gems, semi-precious stones, and ores, and every type of rock. He knew where you could find them. Being about nine years old, I did not know that I was being given a tour by Edward G. Pleva, the department chairman and who I later remembered to be the author of our high school atlas and geography texts in the 1960s.

On another trip, we visited an archeology site where they were digging up Woolly Mammoth bones and an early Indigenous kill site and village. To be standing on the same land that a woolly mammoth had tread upon some 12,600 years earlier made it seem particularly real. I marvelled that little people could bring down such a huge and terrifying beast. My grandfather also took me to the observatory, where we gazed upon the heavens and dreamed of living on the moon.

It is a good thing to have a house that is close to a university. You can see so much more about the world there than almost any other place. My own son at age ten, likewise lived close to a university and we took him to its summer science and computer camps. He knows all the faculties and what kinds of jobs you might get afterwards, and how much you get paid. He wanted to know. Having seen some of life's possibilities and enjoyed himself on campus, he knows what lies ahead. Thanks to my childhood experience, I became the first person in our family to ever attend and graduate from university. And so far, the only one. I had two older aunts who were nurses, and easily the most informed and encouraging people I encountered as a child. I remember that, too. They pointed me toward open fields that I knew nothing about.

I visited London in 1998 and found my old neighbourhood had not changed much. One major difference was that a large apartment block occupied most of the field in front of my old house. Luckily, the forest and river were unchanged. And there were children playing there. The lure of nature was still working.

I also noticed that there was now a paved path leading straight through to a new concrete bridge over the river to Gibbons Park. It made me think that you often find two kinds of people: those who follow paths to get from A to B and those who prefer to roam in open fields. If you follow a path, you will certainly get somewhere. If you play in the field, you will discover things.

Play in fields whenever you can. The path will always be there when you really need it.

CHAPTER THREE

Wave Action

The Cottage at Ipperwash Beach, Lake Huron

Do you recall paint-by-numbers? I knew you would. Our cottage was delivered on a flatbed truck. Hundreds of sticks of wood all neatly precut and carefully numbered were dumped unceremoniously and scrambled on the ground. Building it straight up from the plans might have been easier than sorting out all those pieces, which was my job.

The cottage was a classic log cabin style with a full front veranda, using half-rounded, tongue and groove timbers about fifteen centimetres wide. Mid-1950s style all the way.

An Indian reserve called Kettle Point and Stony Point First Nation was where the lot was, and my father wisely hired a local fellow to help with the construction. As it turned out, he was a very nice man with a large family. I played with some of his children. I had never really met an Indigenous person before, and all that I could find that was different were their last names—like Cabbage. Peculiar. I had played cowboys and Indians for years, and these people didn't live up to their advertising at all. I'm sure my dad tried to explain that TV "Indians" and real Indigenous people were a little different. Except for having a better tan than I could ever manage, I couldn't really find much of a difference between me and them.

On one of the nights when we were building the cottage, a fierce storm blew up on Lake Huron and huge waves pounded in. We only had a tent on the sandy beach, and we had put it up a good thirty metres from the water. Well, the waves got mighty close to the tent, and we moved it up another five metres in the dark. As soon as we had finished that, our Native friend appeared in his pickup truck. He talked to my dad for a moment, and from the look on their faces I could see something awful had happened.

Kettle Point is a long strip of rocks arching a good kilometre out into the lake. A large lake freighter had struck the outer rocks in the storm, and there were at least a dozen crew needing rescue. Could we help? Of course! My dad had good first aid training through Bell Canada, where he worked. We would manage the shore base when the men were brought in. Loading up firewood, food, soup, and our stove as fast as we could, we set off down the dark beach road with the sound of surf roaring all around.

My job was to build a big fire and keep it going, bright and hot. I was only eight years old, and I still remember thinking how important my job was—although throwing wood on the fire was all I really did. I don't know how they did it, but the Native men went out in their skimpy wooden boats through the thrashing waves and rocks in the pitch-black night. Occasionally, I could see their tiny flashlight beams swirling around the waves. When the wind was right, I could hear the ship's bell clanging and even hear faint voices and shouts. My father met the boats at a small cove and helped walk the men over to a sheltered area where my fire burned. Because the boats were so small, only two or three came in at a time. It took two hours, but the Indigenous locals got everyone off safely. Everyone was wet from having to jump into the water before getting pulled into the small boats.

Flames flickered over the most forlorn faces I had ever seen. Wrapped in blankets and sitting close to the fire, the sailors talked only a bit and mostly stared into the fire. My dad kept them warm with coffee, tea, and soup, and the local women came with food. Everything seemed strangely subdued around the campfire. I couldn't understand then why they weren't happy to be alive. They'd just been rescued from the clutches of death. It wasn't what I was expecting.

They were all in shock, of course, but I didn't know what that was. Now, thinking about it, I realize that when their ship went down, they lost their jobs, their paycheques and anything personal they had had on board. And they lost their battle with the sea, which sailors fear the most. Then what?

We were close to an army camp and in the middle of the night, army troop trucks and ambulances appeared all around us. Huge floodlights lit up the entire area and soldiers hurried about rounding up the sailors to take them back to their barracks. For an eight-year-old boy, this was quite a night! Then, as fast as it began, it ended. All the vehicles drove away, and everyone went home into the still-roaring night. And that was my first week at the cottage—before it even went up!

How many times have white folks needed Indigenous guides? Every great explorer needed them, or they'd still be lost on the shores of North America. The local boys became mine. They showed me where the neat stuff was. Little caves, magnetite stones, snake dens, and where the carp came to lay their eggs. Riding carp was one of their pastimes—we're talking little boys and big carp here.

In the sandy, weedy shallows in the slack water area of the point, huge carp, maybe two metres in length, could be found lolling and thrashing the sandy bottom to lay their eggs. If you were quiet and didn't move except like a floating log in the waves, you could get right up beside one and then grab onto its dorsal fin and a front fin and go like stink for a few metres before being thrown off. We thought it was great fun, although I'm sure the carp did not.

When there wasn't much to do outside, I would suggest that we go inside and play some board games or cards or something. I remember that their houses always had their doors wide open but otherwise were little different from my cottage. Both were sparse and simple and smallish for a family to crowd into. I had not realized, at the time, that these were not their summer places but their year-round homes, mostly courtesy of the federal government. Forty years later, I would hear about these old friends of mine again and about the federal government's hand in their lives.

You may remember the Stony Point band in 1995 for occupying and blockading the Pinery Provincial Park and an army base to get these lands back from the federal government which had expropriated them in the 1940s "for a short time during the Second World War." One person was killed by Ontario Provincial Police during that event. I probably played with someone from his family as a child. It is hard to imagine how good these people are and how badly they get treated by our governments.

|||||||||||||||||||||||||||||||||

I get sentimental about the smack of the screen door preceded by that little *sproingy, sproingy* sound of the tightened spring when the door is flung wide open. The door-opener has long since disappeared by the time the door actually swings shut with its memorable *swaap*. You can imagine that sound for yourself. Maybe your screen doors had those little U-shaped door latches that rocked back and forth, adding an extra *kee-thwap*. And the door-opener was invariably out of earshot of "Don't slam the door!"

Thanks to me, our cottage was full of collections. I think most cottages go through this phase at least once a family. Seashells. Seashell bracelets and necklaces. Neat driftwood. Moths that died under the lights. Wildflowers, fresh, dried, pressed, and sacheted. A jar of fireflies by my bed. Frogs and toads and tadpoles. Feathers. Stones. Snakes. I was particularly fond of my snake collection, although I was probably the only one. I had milk snakes, garters, green snakes, and baby water snakes, all nicely stowed in a cardboard box under my bed. I found bugs and frogs for them to eat and generally had a good time with them. I'd let them go again every few days.

Every aunt who came to visit performed the exact same ritual on the snakes. Being overly helpful, my three or four aunts would always volunteer to make the beds in the morning. When they came to my bed for the first time, they would pull back the covers, scream at the top of their lungs and run outside—slamming the screen door—screaming, "BILLYYYYYY!"… and saying, very fast, "You get in here this minute!". Snakes, being cold-blooded, always like a little warmth, and so most of them would make it out their box and up into my bed by morning. They'd be neatly curled up all over the place. Didn't bother me.

My parents didn't seem to be bothered by my collector's habits either. Apparently, though, they never remembered to warn the aunts. All kinds of animals lived in the cottage for a while. My wonderful springer spaniel, Cindy, somehow managed to swim out and capture a young seagull, which she proudly presented to me. It wasn't injured, but it did look frail. I took it back to the cottage, where I knew my mother's maternal instincts would get the better of her. The young seagull had no trouble figuring out who its new mother would be—mine.

Now, young seagulls have a way of obtaining food from their parents. On the parent's beak is a red spot that the young one pecks at to stimulate a regurgitation of the food in the parent's crop. My mother had similar-looking red spots on her legs, I guess. The gull would beeline into her shins from a racing start halfway across the room. Then stand there, looking up expectantly and screeching, as gulls do, wings flapping pathetically at its sides. We learned to keep it well fed. After a few days of this, we let a much fatter bird fly off over the lake. I still have the photo of it.

The summer cottage or cabin is where you learn the really important things in life. Like fishing. Catching your first big one. Learning the truth in the bumper-sticker saying, "A bad day of fishing is better than a good day at work."

One of my best fishing days was when I could see them. We were perch fishing on a clear and warm morning, anchored in ten metres of clear water. The adults were fishing down deep, saying the perch liked it down there where it was cold. Leaning out over the back of the motor and looking up under the boat, I could see several hanging out just under our feet. Dangling my minnow barely in the water over the back, I caught three or four of them in under a minute. Flip. Flip. Flip, into the boat.

"WHAAAAT!?" I said to the staring adults, who hadn't had a nibble. Little kids can be surprisingly adept in unusual ways.

They couldn't believe that the perch were schooling right under our little boat—which even more of them were now that the smell of torn bait was everywhere. After flipping a few more in over the stern, the adults finally sharpened up and began fishing down about a metre instead of ten. We filled the bottom of the boat with the biggest catch anyone had ever seen. We had so much scaling to do that we ended up scaled ourselves.

Mucking about in boats, as Farley Mowat would say, was another favourite. We kept our four-metre fiberglass car-topper in the front yard of the cottage. The five-horse motor and the five-gallon gas can each weighed about the same and were very awkward to carry. My parents had told me that as soon as I could carry the whole works down to the water, tighten the motor on properly, and pull the cord to get it started, I could take it out alone. The agony lasted for several summers. As the fateful summer approached when I was maybe eleven or twelve, my parents added one more condition: and pay for the gas.

Dad let me drive the boat quite a lot. He knew about these things. Somewhat earlier in the summer, my best friend, who had a similar boat and conditions, had made the grade and was bombing around having a great time. My problem was my size—not a very big or beefy kid. Skinny. When I read the ads in the comic books about the ninety-pound weaklings who only needed a set of barbells to look like Mr. Universe, they were talking about me. I made barbells out of two paint cans filled with cement and a piece of pipe between them. It was a crude setup, but I persevered for several weeks, I think.

I had to carry both the motor, and the gas can swinging between my legs, bent akimbo to accommodate the luggage. Lifting the load a few inches off the ground, I would then scamper with little short steps until I could go no more and stop. Repeat until I got to the water's edge. The boat was another problem. It wasn't on a nice little trailer like my friend's; you had to just pick it up or drag it to the water. My dad rolled it onto his back, and off he went with it. When I tried that, I spent some time under the boat, until I dug my way out through the soft sand. I could lift the bow and drag it a bit, but that was all. What to do? What to do? There was my friend out there, circling, leaping over wake waves and racing all over the place. God, what fun! What personal tragedy.

Wanting a trailer so badly, I took apart my little red wagon and lashed together the axles, wheels, and a two-by-four to make a half trailer. The apparatus went under the boat near the balance point and was roped into place. After trying pushing and pulling and turning the boat around to push and pull, I finally settled on pulling on the two handles on the transom—going stern-first toward the water. It was tough getting through so much soft sand with such small wheels, but it was slightly downhill all the way and I followed the harder wet sand whenever I could. I left the boat a metre from the water and went for the motor, the gas, the oars and lifejackets.

My parents were visiting neighbours, I think, and I managed to get all the stuff down to the water without them seeing me do it. With my newfound barbell strength, I tightened the motor clamps as hard as I could. Then I hid the trailer part that had made all the difference and went to tell them I was ready to go!

Parents must enjoy moments like these.

The odd-looking tracks in the sand? Where I had dragged the boat. The wiggly path over wet sand? I couldn't see where I was going, going backwards and all. And could I show them now how I could move the boat, motor and all, into the water? Hmmm. Like a beached whale, the boat was immovable. Perhaps next time I would think to put the boat a lot closer to the water before I put the motor on and put the gas tank in. My dad found a log big enough to put under the boat to roll it to the water, after a couple of tries I managed to heft it into the water.

Now, by this time, I was totally exhausted, and the worst part was yet to come: pulling the start cord on the motor without flinging myself overboard. My dad could just sit there and give a little yank. I had to stand up, brace a foot against the back seat, lean into the motor and then, with both hands on the handle, haul backwards with all my pittance of weight. Often, I couldn't even get the handle to budge out of its holder. If only it would start on the first pull…

Come on, how many things have you ever started on the first pull? Pulling start cords can be one of the most exasperating experiences. I failed. Well, maybe tomorrow. And I had to carry everything back up to the cottage. My dad sympathized with his puny kid and helped improve the trailer piece. That much was OK. I had nightmares about starting the motor. My parents were sure they had nothing to worry about for some time to come. It is important to always be able to start your motor—or else you'll never get back from wherever you went. Nightmares and daymares.

My friend with the boat came by the next morning and I told him all my troubles. This guy was pretty smooth in his boat, and I was interested to learn that he almost always started his motor on the first pull.

"You gotta know when to pull," he said.

For those of you unfamiliar with solving your pull-cord-starting problems, what this kid told me is something you should know. He showed me how to properly prime the gas tank and to squeeze the bulb in the fuel line to get the gas into the motor. Mostly he taught me to listen for the sound of gas squirting in the carburetor. Then he showed me how to set the choke and throttle and to slowly pull the cord to crank the motor past its compression cycle (the hardest to pull against) and just to the start of the exhaust cycle. Then you could really pull on the cord, because you got an easy start and were going full-bore when the compression and firing cycle came up next.

If you do it just right, the motor will start the first or second try—without tearing your shoulder off.

Immediately after breakfast the next day, I hauled everything down to the water again and boasted that I could start the motor on the first try. My parents dutifully came to watch the attempt. I went through the checklist carefully and worked over the motor to get it ready, which drew much attention. Why was I just pulling a little bit on the cord and then letting it go again?

"The motor isn't ready yet. You gotta know when to pull," I said. They nodded.

Kids must really enjoy moments like these.

My friend's advice and instructions were perfect, and it did start the first pull. Instinctively, my parents backed away from the boat, so I slipped the motor into gear and took off. I looked back to see my parents standing knee-deep in the water, their hands on their hips. Another milestone passed. More to worry about. And I had to sweep up at the local mini-putt to earn a little money to pay for gas. But now the waves were mine, all mine!

Every summer at the lake was like that. Something important was accomplished—learning to swim or dive or bead necklaces or fish or run boats or kiss girls and enjoy it for the first time.

Every spring when we arrived to open up, the cottage would seem sparse and lonely. By summer's end, it fit like an old shoe—and smelled like one, too.

To some extent, it was another world. What you learned there was not often of much use back at school in the fall. Many kids didn't go away, and only a few could relate to what my summer had been like. I'd have to wait until the next summer, and it would be a new summer, with new stuff to do.

Having a place with new things to do is what kids like best.

CHAPTER FOUR

Grandparents' Houses

Edward Street, London

Your grandparents' home probably has some of the same features that mine did. Many of the artifacts in it are at least two generations old, some older if you include family heirlooms. My Nana and Papa's little house had lace doilies, fancy teacups, odd kitchen utensils, a 78-rpm record player, velour-covered furniture with huge round arms (all the furniture had feet), deep purple carpets with curvy designs, and a basement that still had a coal bin though the furnace had been replaced. The stairs were almost worn in half from all the traffic up and down.

If you needed a really spooky place to go, I had one.

Their home was a little smaller than a double-wide mobile home, sitting as it did on a ten-metre-wide lot, with a driveway down one side. What you would call a living room they called a sitting room, maybe because it was smaller. One sofa, an armchair, a rocker, and a TV set was all you could fit in and still be able to walk. The dining room was sort of a wide hallway on the way to the kitchen and past two small bedrooms, which hardly held an old double bed and one thin dresser. The closets were so small you couldn't hide in them. Everything was cozy.

A grandparent's house is full of treasures. You find things to marvel at. The distortion of looking through the bowed glass front of the China cabinet. Glass paper weights. War medals. Pocket watches. Lockets and costume jewelry. Fancy hats. The robins' nest in the rose arbour every spring. Old photographs and the stories that went with them. Souvenirs from their travels—a metal Mountie on a horse, a snow globe of Niagara Falls. Collector spoons from all over or collector plates with vivid scenes on them. Many people's homes are full of treasures, but at your grandparents', you get to touch them.

You can even dig up treasure, if you're lucky. One year, after Papa had turned the back garden, I noticed some old metal sticking up and began to dig it out. After completely rearranging the garden dirt, I had found two toy dump trucks and a bulldozer buried there. With a bit of cleaning up, they were just fine. I couldn't imagine how they would have been buried like that by some other family that used to live here. Treasure always makes you wonder.

My family lived in a back summer kitchen room for a year when I was four while our first house was being built a few streets over on Baseline Road. I only vaguely remember it, but I did spend at least ten or twenty weekends and a few weeks every year living at my grandparent's house until I was twelve years old and we moved away from London. I hardly remember the Baseline house at all. My only recollection of that era was going to kindergarten and discovering that our principal's name was Mr. Pickle. Principal Pickle!

My mother was my grandparents' only child, and so my Nana, and my Papa especially, were delighted to have a grandson, and one who adored them. Nana called me "a little imp." Papa called me his grandson. One of the attractions of visiting my grandparents was that they owned a store. When I was a child, the store was part gift shop, tobacconist, school and teacher supplies, toys, a comic book rack, an ice cream freezer and a red Coca-Cola cooler half-filled with water and bottles clinking away every time the cooling pump came on. This was about the best place in the world for a young boy to hang out.

I don't think I would have become a good reader were it not for the comic books and the "classic comics" that were pictorial versions of *Treasure Island, Robinson Crusoe,* and *Peter Pan.* I think if you find appealing literature just lying around in front of you, you pick it up and learn to read it.

One of the more appealing features of grandparents is that they have developed a lot of patience over time. My papa devoted his to his pet budgies, Joey and later, Billy. You could tell when Papa was coming home—the budgie could hear his car over a block away. It would be screeching at the top of its little lungs, "Hello, Gord! Hello, Gord!" until Papa came in the house and went to the bird. His birds adored him, loving him up one side and down the other.

The patience part was that the budgies could really talk. I mean a hundred words or more, poems, little songs and snippets of every soap opera soap commercial from my nana's afternoon TV shows. Papa had a way of getting nose to beak with his budgies and softly talking to them. And the birds sounded just like my grandfather. All too often, a bird would call out to Nana as if it were Gord talking, or she'd think that her soap opera had started, and she'd respond to the sound of it before realizing it was just the bird whistling the show's theme tune.

One of the budgies had to have a rink-side seat during *Hockey Night in Canada*. I don't know what it was—maybe the fanfare, the excitement, the organ music—but the bird had to be there, on the end of the sofa arm. From this vantage point, the bird loved to box and wrestle with your forefinger and leap around. Maybe it was mating with our fingers, I'm not sure. Before the game was over, it would tire out and crawl up to sleep on your shirt collar, its head tucked behind your ear.

Nana's patience was of a different kind. She tended to the details. Counting the coins and bills from the store's till on the dining room table. I helped when I was old enough. I'm sure she did all the paperwork. Papa was the buyer, because he could drive and Nana couldn't, and someone had to be at the store.

My grandparents were people of place. Indigenous in the sense that they were rooted here. Nana spent her early years on a farm, but Papa had grown up in the general neighbourhood and now lived and worked in it. Their store, Stevens' Variety, was in Wortley Village, only a few blocks' walk away. They had had different stores on the same block for over thirty years. Because of the stores, they knew just about everybody and everything about the area.

Oddly, my Nana and Papa appeared to have no good friends. Perhaps rooted people do not have much time available for them. They had family, all of whom still lived in London. With the Marshall side having three brothers, with two, three and four children each, and my mother's side having many aunts and uncles, I remember spending all my visiting time with relatives. People who remain indigenous, like my grandparents, do that. People who are not indigenous visit friends, if they visit at all.

My grandfather lost most if not all his good friends in the First World War. Not being a killing kind of person, he joined the medical corps and became a stretcher-bearer in the trenches in the fields of France. Carrying off his dead and dying friends was his daily routine and inner torture. The last time he saw his last friends was when a mortar shell blew up the people he was walking with, sparing him alone. There was no grief counselling or post-traumatic stress syndrome counselling back then. You just had to carry the pain around your whole life. My grandfather drank until he cried and hugged me on his lap as he told the horrific stories of losing his friends in the war. That is how I remember Remembrance Day.

It was good to have a grandparents' house to marvel at and touch its treasures, to see and hear its secrets, to visit and to be loved. I hope you have had one in your time. Or that you can provide one to your grandchildren.

CHAPTER FIVE

Gateway to Adulthood

North Bay, Ontario

We lived in three houses in "The Gateway to the North," as the entry sign says, even though it is pretty far south by Northern standards. That would be looking down south at Yellowknife from Inuvik in the Northwest Territories, seeing North Bay as a northern suburb of Toronto. I suppose it qualified on the bare grounds that North Bay only had two seasons: winter and construction.

What took our family to North Bay was a transfer and promotion my father received from Bell Canada. These were my early teen years. Where teens grow up has a lot to do with how they grow up.

The first and second houses we lived in were nondescript bungalows in a nondescript newish neighbourhood of houses that all looked the same, except for the different colours some were painted. Three bedrooms and a bathroom down one hall, an L-shaped living and dining room with a kitchen slung across the back. A bleak yard of stubbly grass and a few shrubs. Nothing fancy. We rented the first house for a year while my parents had a new one built on a lot on the next street over. Although spiffy and new, we then only lived there a year before a tantalizing offer came along.

No, I can't tell you anything more about those two bungalows; they were nondescript, like I said, even though my parents helped design and build the second. My parents must have felt that way, too, because they were about to take a big chance. It began with loading everyone into the car and going for a long drive, down along the southern lakeshore of North Bay. My father had been handed a gift horse, had to make his mind up by the next day, and had only one dark evening to check it out—and just a "cruise-by" at that.

After what seemed like a longish drive out of town, down in the motel and fishing lodge strip south of the city, we came to the address we had been given. The driveway was a large U, lined with majestic trees that went by a two-bedroom white cottage and then a stately brick house and large two-car garage.

The grounds were immense, and it was right on the lake. My parents just couldn't say no. The deal was that this place was an old family estate that was now tied up in the courts because the old guy who died hadn't left a will. He wanted his kids to amicably divide things up among themselves. They were into their second year of suits and counter-suits, and it looked like it could go on another year or two yet, my father had been told. We could rent the place *at cost* of taxes and utilities until someone eventually owned it and kicked us out. Little did we think that we would spend three wonderful years there.

There being three young and energetic boys in the family, my parents had made a wise choice. What we had missed seeing on our cruise-by was the thirty metres of cement pier heading out from shore at either end of the property to meet at a small island that had a largish boathouse on it. Inside the triangle was a private and warm beach in the summertime and a helluva good ice rink in the wintertime. It had its own boat launch ramp and that was great in winter too; we could drive a Jeep with a plow on it right onto the ice and clear it off in no time.

For poor folk like us, this was a rich man's heaven. My parents, from working-class backgrounds, had not lived in anything like this before. We were bungalow people. My father had worked his way up in Bell Canada and was now regional manager, making more money than he ever had dreamed. Now he had a rich man's house for a song. The house showed signs of real architectural design (not chosen from a book like ours had been) with glass block light walls, beautiful woods, tile, and recessed everything, and picture windows that looked out over forty kilometres of gleaming lake.

An incredible octopus of a steam heating plant in the basement snorted away during the winter. My father liked it. As soon as he saw it, he pointed out the boiler and water tanks, the pipes and taps and gauges, and he knew what they all did. I soon learned that my father had his "steam ticket," some form of steamfitters' trade qualification, from his teen years. He had earned his ticket while working in the local movie theatres in the late 1930s.

If only theatres today could revisit their past. My dad's job was to run the boilers at the theatre during the movies. When *Scott of the Antarctic* was playing, he'd turn the heat down really low. At intermission, the cigarette girls (you know, the ones in tarty outfits holding a large tray of goodies) would appear with hot chocolate for sale. Of course, for *Lawrence of Arabia*, the heat would get cranked up, and the cigarette girls would have ice-filled soda pop. The westerns and love stories were hot, the war and adventure movies cold. I'm sure the technique helped move a lot of confectionery sales. Compare it to the uniformly cold air conditioning of today's theatres and the stupidly bland pop and popcorn stands in them. This is not progress.

The other thing my dad really liked about this place was the huge workroom in the garage and the fact that we only had one car to put in it. He could build things. We could build things. We had never had a place big enough to set up a tool shop and still have room left over to build something in it. Now, the possibilities were endless. This house was the first of two where we had such space and such potential. (The second came about five years later and was part of a farm.) My dad had pretty good general building skills. He had built a few of his houses, the cottage at Ipperwash, and several small boats when he was much younger. Apart from seeing him build the cottage when I was about eight, I had no real sense of what my father could do, because he had had no place to do it in until now.

The first project was a punt. You know, a peanut shell of a rowboat. You could use it for fishing or duck hunting or just for fooling around in. I think we must have started with the punt, because my dad was a little rusty. We still had the four-metre fiberglass car-topper and the five-horse motor. My younger brother Gary, who was seven or eight at the time, got the most use out of it. The second project was a used boat my parents bought. This was more boat than we had ever had—a five-metre cedar strip runabout with seats for six, a centre console and steering wheel, and a mighty twenty-five-horse motor. Back in 1960, that was pretty good. Except that with cedar strip boats, you had to repair, sand, and refinish them every year whether you liked it or not.

The third project was the best—a sea flea. It was one of those little racing boats with a round front, sort of a hydroplaning design, with room for one person and a gas tank. I remember helping with most of the work of building this boat. Maybe it was because it was my idea—or at least it would be my boat—I kept at the sanding, sanding, sanding, and more sanding and painting. It came out quite well, and I'll tell you more about it soon.

When I took myself down memory lane to remember what was important about that particular house, I was interested to see my thinking revolve around the opportunities that presented themselves because of all that the house, its amenities and location, had to offer. But it made me stop and wonder how incredibly blinkered and shackled we can be by where we live, if it is like a small bungalow in suburbia (or an apartment, I guess), where you have no room to do things or make things. And how much different, richer, and more vibrant your life is when you have tool shops, workshops, garages, playrooms, sewing rooms, lawns you can golf on, boathouses, and a lake that invites you to travel on it, summer and winter. Or fields.

Just down the road… do your teens have a mall or a lake? Do they have boarded-up buildings or beautiful fields? Do they have challenges or monotony? Do they have choices depending on which way you point them when they go out the door?

I want to quickly mention the Minesing Farm (see Chapter Eight), where we lived five years later, which also had a large tool shed where we worked on farm machinery, lawn mowers, and little broken-down motorcycles. We invented weeding attachments, designed trailers for snowmobiles and hopped up little mopeds to race around the cornfield. My younger brother Gary got so much experience in this shed working with our dad (I was off at university by this time) that he went on to become a Class A mechanic. Even my youngest brother, Greg, put in a lot of time out there, but his interest was more electrical. Today, he installs and maintains sophisticated alarm and fire suppression systems.

I wonder how many kids grow up with dads or moms who do know how to make things, who know how to enjoy life but who don't live in a house where they can do that. Developers don't build houses like that one anymore. They haven't for over fifty years. Now we get places to sit in our houses—the home movie theatre room, the home office and the hot tub. We have become soaker-uppers instead of builders and doers because of what our houses are designed for. When the bungalow suburbs sprang to near-life in the 1950s, they were touted as models of easy living. True enough. *Boring* living would be a better description, though.

By chance, I read in the newspaper two reports on research books that had just been published. One book addressed how well the children from families with active fathers turned out compared to fatherless children. The other book looked at the particular problems that children without dads had. About one in five children lack an active dad in their family. Most never had one to begin with, and some have only a dad in name. The uninvolved father is all too common. It's just happenstance more than not. How can we do better? It takes a lot of work and time to raise children. Having two parents (could also be two moms or two dads) makes it so much easier to be with your children to see to all their needs. Life is complicated.

After thinking about housing and how it has really changed over the past sixty years, I must lay at least some of the blame on developers and urban planners of the recent past and present for building houses and suburbs in all our cities that fail to address some basic fatherly needs. Fathers need special places to spend time with their sons and daughters. Workshops, games rooms, playing fields, small lakes and rivers. We don't build or create nearly enough of them. It's hard enough to find a good park in a sea of high-rises let alone places to explore, which challenge you.

Houses are far from work. Hours are lost to commuting every day—hours that should be spent at home with the family. Our current housing and working patterns are contributing to the strains on the family, and often both parents are working. Men can be more domestic, and should be really involved in domestic life, too. To want to be a stay-at-home domestic father is a good thing, but still rare. You see the problems men face trying to be good fathers in today's crazy world.

But maybe for both parents, it's about room to do things with your kids. We should be designing our apartment buildings with more than a common room to rent. We need a workshop, a sewing room, a games room, a playroom. We are missing the time parents and kids spend together. As the healthy communities coordinator for the City of Coquitlam some years ago, people were telling me that they needed amenities like that near them. The city was building big rec centres that were too hard to get to from the outer neighbourhoods. *What about smaller rec centres all over the place*? they asked. What about neighbourhoods?

||||||||||||||||||||||||||||||||

I don't think that I saw the insides of the houses of half my friends. There were usually four of us—Brian, Andy, Bob, and Keith. Having more hectic households than ours, they liked being at our place much more. Rainy summer days, we hunkered down in the rec room and played rummy and hearts and bridge when we could manage it. We had stamp collections and got them out, had day-long trading parties, dreamed of their growing value. On sunny summer days, we worked part-time jobs, water-skied, swam and dove off our boathouse island. Yeah, it was a tough life.

One thing about this arrangement that always struck me was that my parents knew my friends quite well, but my friends' parents barely recognized me, or the others, on the street. I hardly ever got to look at their lives as they lived them at home. On the rare occasion I did get a glimpse into their home life, it was never what I imagined it would be. For the most part, my friends were much better behaved at our place than they were at home. They talked back to their parents but would patiently sit through one of my mother's tongue-lashings or lectures. They fought with their brothers and sisters, but we never seemed to squabble. It was a mystery.

A big, spacious house on the lake like this one invited parties. My parents inevitably hosted many—too many, sometimes. Weekends brought dinner guests, cocktail parties before other events, and just plain day-long parties. This was the heavy cocktail era, when executive types tried to drink each other under the table. It would be ten years before my parents recovered from all that entertaining. I guess that is a liability when you have a house for entertaining. I'm glad I was too young for that.

Again, my parents had far more parties and guests than they ever had invitations to other people's homes. They often talked about wanting to see how so-and-so lived and wishing they'd get more invitations. Unfortunately, it seems that when you have a big place that lends itself to entertaining, you do a lot more entertaining than people who do not have suitable homes for it.

||||||||||||||||||||||||||||||||

When you live on a lake in a small Northern community surrounded by bush, you are inevitably drawn into hunting and fishing. Fishing we knew, but hunting was something that we had not tried. Duck hunting was a local favourite because we were so close to good marshes. Just hop in your boat, take your decoys and shotguns, and head out. To fifteen-year-old boys, there are few better adventures to have. I had a close friend from the first neighbourhood we had lived in who had grandparents who lived just down the road from our lakeshore house. Brian came down as often as he could. We both had boats and water skis, and we spent a great deal of time together.

One grey fall Saturday morning, we set out for our favourite duck marsh, a river delta with wide channels cutting through swaths of tall rushes and grasses. A few islands protruded above, and we had claimed one of them and set out our decoys. There were only a few other hunters out and we knew why. Within two hours, the weather had deteriorated badly, and a black line of clouds drew up over the horizon. The other hunters packed up and left. We knew there would be lots of ducks coming in to ride out the storm, so we stayed put. It made sense to us at the time.

Then we started thinking. Maybe we should go after all. Beat the storm home. There would be other duck hunting days. We couldn't ride it out; we hadn't brought enough food, and we had no blankets or other comforts. So, as we saw white-capped waves begin to build ahead of the black clouds, we hauled out our decoys and headed straight into the approaching storm just as the ducks were coming in to avoid it. As we had feared, the storm bore down on us far more quickly that we had hoped. We were out in it, and there was no turning back. We spun sideways on top of huge wave crests. Up and down the rollercoaster waves, with our bums being hammered one moment and rising off our seats the next. White-capped waves suddenly rose up beside us, slapped us sharply in the face, and then almost threw us over.

We were scared as hell. We would say it out loud. "I'm scared." Which would make us feel better, somehow.

We had been out in some rather rough weather before, but nothing like this. We had Brian's boat this time. It was another cedar strip boat, a little smaller than ours (a Powassan, for those of you who know such things), with a fifteen-horse motor, tiller-steered. Brian was driving, and I was up front to give us the best balance for fighting the growing waves. Perched up front, I could read the water better and tell Brian what lay ahead.

Unfortunately, we found we had to run broadside against the big waves to make our way home, about five nautical miles up the shoreline from our hunting spot. Running broadside to waves is not entirely wise, so we also ran straight into them a bit and then out of them at an angle. By this time, the waves were a good two metres or more high, with very small troughs in between. Nippissing was a shallow lake on that side, and the waves were tall and tightly packed.

After hollering at each other for fifteen minutes about how best to take the waves, we had a good system worked out. When we saw fairly flat water, we raced out across it then took the first big trough we found and stayed right in it as long as we could. We had to keep a sharp eye for waves cresting over us and into the boat. Just before that happened, we would deke ahead or behind it, or if that failed, turn straight up and over it and bang down on the other side.

We mastered the wave-riding after a while, and realized that we were no longer scared, that we were in the angry fist of a storm and we were having a whale of a time. The testosterone was running high. As each monster wave approached or broke near us, we shouted curses and taunts at it and then we deftly avoided it and cruised on. We were bold. We knew we could survive if we just kept our wits about us.

Arriving home, we had great trouble making it into our pier with the bounding waves boring into the entranceway, but we made it. Our respective parents and grandparents were completely overawed that we had survived that storm and the huge waves. People were watching for us, but no one had seen us until we had come in close to the pier. It scared the hell out of our parents, and I think we were grounded for a while, but that didn't matter. Brian and I knew we had faced death, fought back, and won. For us, it was a definite step up on the ladder to adulthood, something that you needed to know about yourself when you faced real danger again.

And I did encounter similar dangers on that lake. Duck hunting again—but this time I was on a small water taxi that was headed down the French River at the south end of the lake from Sturgeon Falls on the north side. The old boat, maybe nine metres long, carried a dozen people. This time there were several Indigenous women with a few children each, an older fellow, and three of us teenagers. Since it was October, the sun had set by the time we started out. Halfway across the lake, we felt the temperature drop abruptly and the winds pick up. And then came the snow. Boating in darkness, in wind, in snow, were three things that I didn't feel very comfortable doing. You start to think long and hard about your life.

We were close to the most hazardous part of the trip, Canoe Pass, the entrance to the French River from the side we were approaching. Canoe Pass was an apt name for a narrow channel between two cliff-faced islands at the mouth of the river. For a kilometre or so in front of the islands, there was shallow water, sandy shoals and rushes and weeds as far as you could see. A channel had been dredged straight through to Canoe Pass. It was marked by cans (forty-five-gallon drums) painted black or red or green. There were also poles with fluorescent markers so you could sight down the channel at night. As we approached the mouth of the channel, the water taxi's searchlight died. In stunned blackness, the pilot throttled back. Panic buttons went off inside my chest.

Even through the thickly falling snow, we had been able to see the channel markers and the stretches of rushes in the search light's beam. Now all we saw was utter darkness as we pitched back and forth in the waves. The taxi's pilot couldn't do much, because he had to try to keep the boat steady without knowing where he was. After a quick talk around the cabin, it came down to me knowing more about wiring and lights than anyone else. I dove under the dash to inspect the switch and the wiring, following it carefully to the roof. It seemed fine.

This was going to be my first—and maybe last—chance to be a hero. The pilot had a spare bulb, and gave it to me, along with a screwdriver, some tape, and a knife, in case I found a wire broken.

With the boat pitching in the snow storm and icing up, blacked out except for a flashlight that I had to try to carry and hang on to the boat at the same time, I had to crawl up onto the cabin roof, find the searchlight, inspect it, open it with a screwdriver, check the bulb— and YES! It was just a burned-out bulb, and we had light again, just in time to avoid grounding into the rushes. All I could see up there was a dizzying blizzard of snow evaporating into the black water beneath. And dimly, just a few fluorescent markers.

As we almost surfed waves through Canoe Pass, with three metres' clearance on either side, I realized, as did everyone else, that we were almost goners that time. Of course, I wanted to let the pride roll as people thanked me for fixing the light when one of the Indigenous women said that she knew I could do it because her spirit guide can always cross the lake safely and so she was never afraid that I would fail. The pilot agreed. I could now see that he was Indigenous, too. He said that's why he always felt safe when she was on board. I didn't mind having the extra help.

||||||||||||||||||||||||||||||||

I won't bore you with fishing stories, because I really didn't do much fishing. Water-skiing and just racing around was about all I wanted to do on the water at that age. And so, the building of the sea flea was a very special event in the neighbourhood. Garages and workshops have a special kind of light in them, usually slightly amber from bare bulbs reflecting off wood beams and walls. And off heaps of sawdust on the floor. I can remember being in there, working away, more than I can remember being anywhere else in that house or on its grounds.

The sea flea was finally ready. I painted it red and white, and even waxed it thoroughly, before launching it.

Of course, my dad had to try it out first to see if it was sea-worthy and how well it would behave. He was a bit heavy for it and its little five-horse motor. It took him quite a while to get the bow to lie down and really go. The sea flea is a planing boat, entirely. It starts out by pointing straight up, and as you gain speed, the nose comes down, and off you go, skippitty-skip. It stops the same way—the nose goes straight up, you have backwash over the transom to be careful of, and then it flattens out. You want to do that part just right, too, or you could sink yourself in a moment.

A sea flea is rated to have a five-horse motor because it is just a little thing, barely two and half metres long, a little more than a metre wide, maybe thirty centimetres deep, and light as a feather. As soon as all parents were otherwise occupied, we clamped on Brian's fifteen-horse motor. Just for fun, you know. The motor was so heavy on the back of the sea flea that it would have sunk had not two of us held up the stern until the driver got it started and took off, with us letting go at the last instant. We didn't want to think of what would happen if it stalled out in deep water. We ran it right into the sandy shore when we stopped so it wouldn't sink.

Geez, that boat went like a bat out of hell! We figured it went somewhere between forty-five and fifty-five nautical miles an hour based on how fast we could cross the forty-kilometre lake and come back. It was really tricky to handle at such speeds, but we never knew you couldn't go that fast, so we did.

Well, that didn't last too long. One day, as Brian was roaring past our boathouse, I heard a loud noise, like a chainsaw revving, and saw the sea flea come to an abrupt stop with the motor still wailing away. And it didn't sink. Brian shut the motor down and I lit out in our boat to rescue and tow him in. When we tilted his motor up, we saw that the entire lower part was gone. A short way away, we saw the semi-submerged log he had hit—he had cleared it in the sea flea but caught it square with the shaft of the motor. Good thing, too. Remember that the sea flea would have sunk with the whole motor still there. Boy, did we get heck.

Back to the five-horse motor. Even that could give you thrills and laughs. A local friend, Andy, hadn't had a chance to try it out, and though a bit of klutz, he figured he could handle it. We carefully went through the start-up routine. Put it in neutral, twist the handle to the START position, pull the cord, idle down, get yourself set and braced, put it in gear, lean forward and crank up the throttle. The bow should rise up and you lean on it. Down it comes and *zoom*, off you go.

So, Andy went through the steps. He put it in neutral, set the handle in the START position, pulled the cord and started the motor, and idled down. He got himself properly braced and cranked on the throttle. With the motor roaring and Andy going nowhere and looking puzzled, we shouted at him, "Idle down!! You have to put it in gear before you—"

But he only heard the last part and realized the step he had missed.

He leaned back and threw the gear lever forward. Five tearing horsepower hit the propeller. Leaping clear out of the water, the sea flea went one way, and Andy flipped back the opposite way. Like a launched missile, the sea flea stopped in mid-air and came straight down, promptly garbled, and sank. Andy did the same. We laughed so hard our stomachs ached. We fished them both out of the shallow water. Andy was unhurt and would never get in the sea flea again. At least now we knew how the sea flea got its name. It took two days to tear down the five-horse motor and get it going again. But it was worth it. For years, we would laugh uncontrollably at the mention of the leaping sea flea.

By the third summer, we were using the motorless sea flea as a surfboard on the big rollers that came in during storms. An era had passed in our short but speedy, brave, and comical lives. Teenagers. Sadly, I have no pictures of this house, as it was torn down some time ago. My friend Brian still lives in a house a few doors down on this beach of Lake Nipissing. I understand that waterfront homes are special places especially for growing children. My wife had similar growing up experiences at her family's summer cottage where challenges to try new things beckoned. You swam, you canoed, you boated, you built sandcastles and discovered the creatures that lived around you. Not all of us get these opportunities but Canada is a land of lakes, so many of us do. Living by the seashore, or a lake or pond also lets you read the weather and the seasons. Every change tells a story of what is to come.

CHAPTER SIX

New Worlds, New Friends

Dollard des Ormeaux, Montréal, Québec

When you move to new places, there are some general rules as to what you can expect. I would have to admit that these rules don't always stand up, but they usually do. If you move into an old, established neighbourhood where the neighbours have lived a long time, newcomers like you can be viewed with skepticism. On the other hand, if a neighbourhood or community is new, so are the people who live there, and you can get to know them much faster.

There is a certain culture shock moving from a small Northern town in Ontario to a cosmopolitan centre like Montréal. First, there is the French-Canadian culture and its 350 years of tradition in Québec. Then there are the immigrant communities—Italians, Greeks, West Indians, Jews from Europe, and a host of others. A walk down a Montréal street on a warm summer's evening was a world tour of food aromas wafting out front doors and open windows. The music and talking that sounded so unusual at one house would be replaced by sounds and language that were equally rich and new at the next. And colour. I had never seen such colours in all my life—on houses, on people, on everything. People were quite friendly, and you could stop and talk and learn fascinating stories about these people. Living on a downtown street could soon broaden your worldview—well beyond Montréal and Canada. I didn't live on one of those streets, but some six years later, I would frequently stay with friends who did.

Montreal—indeed, all of Québec—is more European than anything else. Music influences come as much from Europe as they do from the United States. Jazz fusion, popular in Montreal, is kind of a rock and classical-pumped jazz form that seems to be found nowhere else except in Europe. Groups like ABBA from Sweden, the Chieftans from Ireland, Genesis from England, and others from France and Germany were in town playing sold-out concerts. Québec's own musicians played to huge crowds. Diane Dufresne, a Madonna fifteen years before Madonna, strutted to her sexy, no-holds-barred rock while Beau Dommage soared where Fleetwood Mac later ventured. You don't hear the Quebec music scene in English Canada. Why didn't we hear of these musicians in the rest of Canada? I think it must be English snobbery or thinking that the French lyrics wouldn't go over in English Canada or that the French groups were just too damn good.

I was sixteen when I arrived in this new city in the early 1960s. Here, teenage culture was entirely different. In a small town like North Bay, Ontario, which I had just left, change was slow. No one tried new things or new clothes, in case they stood out too much. Most people living there had lived there all their lives, cliques of friends were tight and cool to newcomers, and you could only do what there was to do in a small town. That was it and no more. Montréal multiplied what you could see and do and learn a hundredfold.

Dollard des Ormeaux, a newish suburb, lingered on the outskirts of fast-growing Montréal. Almost everyone who lived there were themselves newcomers, just like me. Most fortunately, the high school I went to was also new, brand new, fittingly named Riverdale High, the same high school in the popular Archie comics. Coincidence? My first living arrangements were also brand new to me.

My father received yet another job transfer from Bell Canada and we were to move here from North Bay within three months. Since school started in September, I wanted to move on quickly and get it over with. On a whirlwind trip to Montréal with my father, we quickly chose a likely neighbourhood to move to. With some luck and quick friendship, one of my father's new co-workers offered to board me for a few months until our family moved. My father lived and worked in downtown Montréal while I boarded in the suburbs and my mother and two younger brothers packed up the house in North Bay, moving out in December.

Being a first-time boarder in someone else's house is a real eye-opener for a young fellow. Here was a house that looked like so many I had lived in, but the smells were all wrong, the sounds peculiar, and the house rules different. These kind folk were younger than my parents, and they had a three-year-old daughter who was delightful. I remember feeling quite out of place at first. How can you be yourself in such foreign surroundings?

After a few weeks, I did find my place. It was just much smaller than I was used to. Living in someone else's house as a boarder limits your experience of it. There were parts I didn't go into and times I didn't leave my room. I couldn't really have friends over or do anything loud. Most of the life I had just left behind was impossible to replicate here.

The couple's three-year-old daughter became a best friend. Obviously very bright and inquisitive, she spent as much time with me as she could. Playing with her train set, she asked me how it worked. Patiently, she asked me precise questions about every aspect of it, and I lost her only when we got to the theory of electrons and how magnetic motors worked. She delighted in knowing everything she could. I liked that, because I am kind of like that, too. As a boarding student, you can only develop so much of a relationship with a three-year-old, however, and I was itching to be able to get out and learn more about my new surroundings.

When my family finally moved into a house a few blocks away, I was relieved, to say the least. Now I could be *me* again—whoever that was. Moving from one house to another was bad enough, but we moved from a house on a lake to the centre of endless suburbia in a newer part of a huge city. No boating, no skiing, no fishing… no one there who knew who I was.

That's one of the things about living in different houses in different cities that you soon learn: everything is new, including who you can be. You can refocus on who you want to be with the opportunity of a fresh start. I had not moved too often by this time in my life, but I was already getting the hang of reinventing myself in each new place. No one here knew my shortcomings, the embarrassing moments and other indiscretions I'd rather forget. They didn't know the good stuff, either, but that was fine.

It was easy to meet people and make new friends. We all needed new friends. There were no cliques in the high school, I think partly because we had to wear uniforms. The girls wore blue tunics and the boys grey flannels, a white shirt and tie, and a sweater. Our new high school had no traditions or culture to live up to. Indeed, we got to invent some of the traditions we wanted to see the school have. We were involved and encouraged to talk a great deal. School was different there, too. Teachers were more open, ready to discuss heady subjects and tackle sensitive issues. In this open atmosphere, it was easy to pick out the people you wanted to meet and befriend. And I had lots of friends before too long.

I don't really know why, but I spent a lot of time in my new friends' houses during the two years I lived there. Maybe because everyone was new here, invitations were more freely offered. Maybe it was because we were all teenagers who couldn't stand being alone with ourselves for more than half an hour. Maybe because everyone was groping for new friends in a new place. Maybe it was because we teenagers fell in and out of love every three months. All our houses seemed to be open to drop-by visitors—mostly teenagers. I got to know all the parents of my friends in this suburb. And our parents met others in the neighbourhood through us.

A few friends have told me that there are many similarities in this house story with people who live on armed forces bases. Transferred every few years and having to start all over again—in small towns, big cities, and different cultures, armed forces families always live this changing life. Although there is much to be said about being rooted in one place, you sure miss seeing how other people live in this interesting country of ours. In high-turnover areas, you meet a lot of people you would never meet in any other situation.

Dollard des Ormeaux was a split-level city. You can usually tell exactly how old a suburb is by its housing style. Unfortunately, almost all the houses reflect the house style trend when the subdivision was built. There are suburbs of bungalows, ranchers, split-levels with one garage door out front, and the modern two-storey box with a double garage door for a front. The song "Little Boxes"—"ticky tacky boxes"—by Malvina Reynolds comes to mind.

Unspectacular houses leave a neighbourhood with a feeling of sameness wherever you go. It's easy to get lost, because so little stands out. *Drab* is a description that fits. But it is interesting how appearances can be deceiving. There was more life there than I'd ever encountered, all happening indoors. I would live in other places that looked just like this neighbourhood, but the life was entirely different. Everyone living here was from somewhere else and might soon be moving elsewhere before long. You had a sense of *enjoy it while you can.*

One special house I remember was the teen house. It was old, red brick, I think, and right on the main street of the suburb. I have no idea where it came from or who really managed it, but the local teens had their own house all to themselves. I can't ever remember seeing an adult in it. Working on an honour system, it just worked. It had sofas, a pop machine, a snack bar box, a stereo that we could play our own records on, and a pool room. And, of course, posters and wild painted things on the walls.

I remember that we had sort of a management committee and made our own decisions about rules, how much pop to buy, what needed cleaning and whose behaviour needed to be dealt with. After school, evenings, and weekends, you could just drop in, flop down, and have a good time.

I really wish I knew how that house got going and who owned it. The city's recreation department? A society? Just some person who rented it to us? Was it an abandoned house we just sort of squatted in? Whatever it was, we took care of it like it was our own. No vandalism, no hassles, no fights. Girls and guys came, though I remember some of the girls' parents not being too keen on it.

Necking parties were common. A few couples would all go to someone's house to make out. It seemed safer with others around— so you wouldn't go too far, you know. It wasn't always successful, this being the dawn of the sexual revolution and the permissive age. The Catholics among us were still mostly repressed, but everyone else was moving into new territory. Back in North Bay, the only place you could neck was in your parent's borrowed car on some lovers' lane or lookout, and only after a big date or dance. Here, it was an after-school activity.

By grad night, which happens at the end of Grade 11 in Quebec, all restrictions were dropped. It was expected to be an all-nighter. Some parents threw the cocktail parties before the grad ceremony and dance. Another would host the breakfast party. In between, we rented limousines and spent the night up on Mont Royal overlooking downtown Montréal and waiting for the sun to rise, all the while keeping ourselves quite busy.

Drinking at parties was commonplace, but very few ever got drunk. The drinking age in Québec is eighteen and beer and wine are sold in every corner store to whomever looks almost eighteen (or older). Most of the drinking would be at parties at someone's home and under the supervision of their parents, even if most of the kids were under eighteen. Since it wasn't such a big deal, it wasn't a big deal, I guess.

My family only spent two years there. It seemed more like four or five. I earnestly took up skiing, hopping on the rented bus with the school ski club and heading up to the Laurentians in the early morning, returning late at night. In the summer, I worked as a recreation director at a lake in the Laurentians, teaching water-skiing and sailing to city slickers. I could use my skills, find my passions! Life was good.

Once again, the transfer notice came, and we were packing up, saying goodbyes. Here, I found that moving to a new house in a new place can be the best thing that happens to you. So, I was looking forward to the next move.

CHAPTER SEVEN

Small Window Frames

Barrie, Ontario

Moving from the liberal and cosmopolitan dynamo of Montréal to the small city of Barrie, Ontario was like moving back in time. Only two years had passed. I had caught a glimpse of my destiny in Barrie while visiting my old friends back in North Bay after having lived in Montréal for a year. Montréal was bright with fashion. The Quiet Revolution was underway, and clothes were the banner.

Paisley and madras were in, in deep burgundy, often worn with a grey Beatles jacket, like the one this hip Montréal teenager had acquired. As soon as I stepped off the train in North Bay, my friends greeted me with whistles and catcalls. They would not be the last I heard. Black pants, blue sweaters, and white shirts were still the only attire among middle-class teens here. Jeans were fine, and the tougher guys wore white T-shirts with black leather jackets and Wellington boots with clickers on them. With a pack of Export "A's" up their left sleeve. Among these teens one Friday night shone a sole bright, burgundy light such as the town had never seen. Or heard of. Even the local press and TV hadn't bothered to cover fashion trends in the big cities.

Guys in low-slung rumbly cars cruised the main drag, often returning for a second look and a whistle at me. It was a gruelling weekend visit, because I had proudly packed nothing but mix-and-match burgundy and grey clothes in all the latest designs. I could not escape my new image.

Barrie was like that, except that I had to *stay* there. My father was transferred to Barrie just as I entered Grade 13, a rather useless year, as they covered the same material in Grade 11 in Québec. By the time teens hit their last year of high school, almost everyone belongs to one group of friends or another, and there often isn't room for a newcomer. Especially one far more hip than the locals.

The only real friend I had in high school was another newcomer, who had recently been kicked out of an expensive private school. He was a smart-ass, which is someone who is really smart but not being challenged to use those smarts. The public school system couldn't really cope with him either. We stuck it out together as friends, and our science and math teachers seemed to understand our plight, assuring us that getting to university would change everything.

The house my family lived in was a nondescript bungalow in a suburb—sound familiar? I cannot really remember ever having a friend over to it, and I don't think I ever went into anyone else's house, except maybe the front doorway, picking up a date. Here, the newer suburbs looked like they did in Montréal, only smaller, just a few blocks. Barrie was cold and closed compared to Montréal. Where once I found life beyond my imagining, here I found next to nothing. I couldn't wait to leave.

Moving teenagers in their high school years is not a good thing. Their circle of friends is so important to their wellbeing. I should say that my two younger brothers fared better than I did. They are seven and twelve years younger than I am, so they had different things to deal with. Fortunately for me, we were only there a year before we moved out to the country. I think I had about three dates and remember being alone more than anything. Trying to meet others just never seemed to work out. I carried around a catch-22. Since I was alone to begin with, no one wanted to spend any time with me.

Barrie girls were afraid to be exciting. And their parents warned them about guys like me. Jocks were the only guy game in town. I wasn't one of those. Many people I met had never left town in their entire lives. They didn't seem to think it would be worth it—or their parents never let them.

I left the house in Barrie for any reason I could. During the summer, the best escape was out on the highway, going north to "The Pav" in Orillia or south to Yorkville Avenue in Toronto.

The Pav (Pavilion) should have a movie made about it. When I encountered it in 1966, it was rather run down, but it still had its charm. It was a summer dance hall in a city park on a lake. Today's cities would never consider such a thing. White clapboard exterior, square and squat, with large windows opening onto a porch all the way around, this old dance hall had it all.

Inside, there were sitting booths all around the horse-hair-sprung dance floor. Behind those booths was a hallway and more booths on the back walls. Each booth sat six people, a carload, so the group could stay safely together. A refreshment bar and washrooms were at the back, and the stage was at the front. The Pav was the focus of the new rock and roll wave sweeping North America and Britain. David Clayton Thomas, Lighthouse, Rompin' Ronnie Hawkins, Ugly Ducklings, Stitch in Tyme—bands that were so good people stopped dancing just to marvel.

The Pav was used to this kind of thing. Since it was built in the 1930s, it had seen all the big bands and big stars. Their posters were still on the walls—Tommy Dorsey, Guy Lombardo, Glenn Miller, Patsy Cline, B.B. King… The Pav was made entirely of wood, all of which was its natural colour inside. A golden glow, dampened sound, creaks everywhere, and beams and posts and pillars. Soft and solid all at once.

Also, in Orillia there was a house that boasted something solid and unique. What kind of house does a humourist live in? I guess that's what draws us tourists in to see the summer house of Stephen Leacock, a great Canadian humourist, for those of you who may not have heard of him. *Sunshine Sketches of a Small Town,* about an Orillia slightly twisted by his wit and whimsy, can be glimpsed in his house overlooking Lake Couchiching. Bright green chestnut trees bloomed out front and over a white archway and trellis leading to the large veranda and front door of the white cottage. Once inside the door, you'd be surrounded by natural wood, mostly yellow cedar—wood floors, wood walls, wood ceiling, wood staircase, wood cupboards in the kitchen, wood fridge. Wood, wood, wood, wood. Much of the furniture was of wicker, including many wicker lamps with silk tops, fringes, and tassels. Tiffany lampshades, too. Library shelves were everywhere. Where you would put a grand piano or a great sofa, there was a huge writing desk and chair. Then, as if to tempt fate, there was a fireplace in almost every room.

With the golden glow of fires and sunsets on the lake to light his golden wooded home, Leacock's warm humour must have been infused into him by his house. Or perhaps his house was a reflection of his mind, and that's the way he wanted it. All of this brings up the question of—can we build ourselves houses that are perfectly designed to help us express or be who we are? What kind of influence can a house or space have on us anyway? The Pav had an inviting dancefloor with a springiness that said dance. Leacock's home said think and write warm thoughts.

CHAPTER EIGHT

The Charms of Country Living

Edgehill Acres, Minesing, Ontario

The summer before I went to university, my parents sold the house in Barrie and moved to a four-hectare farm about twenty-five kilometres outside of town, on the outskirts of Minesing. There we were, on a curve of Highway 26 which connects Barrie to Wasaga Beach and Collingwood. With a population of maybe a few hundred, one sometimes-open garage, a general store, two churches, and an apiary as the only industry, Minesing is easily missed as you drive by on the way to somewhere else.

The two-storey, high-peaked-roofed, red brick farmhouse was like one of a thousand others in Ontario's farm country. My father began by converting the garage into a rec room—this time British, Tudor-pub style. Behind the house was a four-bay drive shed and then a medium-sized barn with a chicken coop on the front side. My parents were going to be gentleman farmers, truck farmers, hobby farmers, or something like that. They had no idea.

Sheep farming sounded good. Cuddly little lambs. Maybe market garden vegetables. How about poodles? Why not? The romance of hobby farming is hard to elude, especially if you haven't tried it yet.

My parents did new things then. Sometimes they'd get icky up to their armpits, helping to turn wrong-way lambs around during birth. An orphaned lamb would be bumbling about the kitchen, getting bottle-fed. Fortunately, an old sheep herder helped them out of that one. To get an orphaned lamb to be accepted by a new ewe, you first had to tie a kerchief around the ewe's neck for a day. Then you put it on the lamb. When the ewe smelled the approaching lamb, she'd assume it was hers and adopt it. The same trick works on all kinds of animals, including kittens who'd nurse from dogs, which we later discovered.

Instead of dinner on the dining room table, you found a cardboard carton of fluffy yellow chicks to tend. Instead of sitting around watching TV, you were disking a corn field on a bumpy tractor. Instead of hanging out, you were banging in fence posts. Instead of grooming yourself, you were clipping wiggly little puppies. Instead of shopping at the butcher, you were trying to cope as you watched even your favourite lambs go to slaughter and come home as lamb chops and roasts. Instead of lifting weights, you were scuffling in a hot dusty field, lifting bales of hay onto the hay wagon, repeating the process from the wagon up to the loft of the barn.

This made weightlifting seem really tame by comparison. First, you couldn't quit until you were done. Second, you had to do it before it rained, no matter what.

Have you ever tried chasing chickens back into the coop? Rounding up sheep without a good sheepdog? Boy, a farm can keep you busy and in good shape. Then you notice that the chickens and sheep will come in at dark anyway. Just don't try to move them before they are good and ready. The things you must learn about farming.

Crops are always a problem. Cucumbers for instance. Good work for philosophers. Lots of time to think, picking bushels full every day. We stupidly had so many, we had to sell to Bick's.

While attending university in Peterborough, I spent a few summers, my winter and spring holidays, and a birthday or two at the farm. During the summers, I also worked at summer jobs to help pay for university. One of those was a construction job at a new museum in Wasaga Beach. For Tuesday, Wednesday, and Thursday nights, I lived out of my little van, which I arranged to park at the local zoo. For companionship, just a few metres away, was the pride of lions. No need for an alarm clock there. At sunrise, lions either yawn loudly or clear their throats vociferously, or just talk to one another. It is louder than one of those boom box car stereos. I also learned not to eat in front of them; that made them noisy, too.

It was my occasional visits to the farm that would leave a deep impression on me. Something was always happening that was utterly different from the academic life of a student. At university, you studied the growth of agribusiness and heard about its riches. Here, you saw the family farm and the rich life that afforded farmers. At the cafeteria, you ate burgers and fries. Here, you knew what it took to get the steer and potatoes onto your plate.

If you live in the city, weather can be an inconvenience, at worst an annoyance. It doesn't rule your life like it does when you farm in the middle of nowhere. You have to plow when the field is dry enough. You have to plant at the right time of year. You have to harvest before the frost. You have to irrigate if there's a drought. You have to sit tight for days on end during snowstorms, sometimes with your power out and animals to care for. You look out your window every chance you get, to see what chance you have of doing what needs to be done. This is how a farmhouse frames your life.

One November, I came home over the Remembrance Day long weekend. The leaves had fallen, leaving fall hanging in the air. A golden glow from the low sun filled the countryside. I was so impressed by what happened that day that I wrote a prose piece about it that was published in the literary journal at university. I still have it. Written in about 1969, I repeat it here—

November Day

At about noon, I looked out my window to the barn, the sheep mulling behind the barn and all the valley below it. An undulating valley of neat farms rolled down like a river without a current. I have never seen anything so tranquil as farmland before the first snow.

I grabbed my green coat and flung open the screen door—its loud clap absorbed by the wall of silence of still fall air. The orange wafer sun slowly became blanketed by dark November clouds. As I made my way to the gate I was struck by the sharp shadows of sun and cloud-blotched fields mottled before me. The air felt warm and dry but as the shadows moved toward me, the wind picked up, softly at first.

As near to the middle of the hay field as I could get, I lay down. I rustled there for a while amid cheek-tickling tips of grass and the dankness of dry leaves. Overhead, one small dark cloud with a hole in it had transformed the sun into a rusty ball with silver-fringed cotton around it. I finally succeeded in lying perfectly still. Not a sound. A breeze puffed, died and puffed again. A trace of hay stole a sniff from the pure air. The sun warmed my face a moment then a cloud passed and it was cool, then warm again.

I stood up and looked to the wood lot. The evergreens seemed to mock the naked black deciduous trees. The surrounding brush, like jumbled barbed wire, seemed to throw up these black trees to scratch the sky with their crooked fingers. To hold back the approaching storm.

It turned cold of a sudden. I zipped up my jacket and my hair flew about. I looked at the fields I had planted and harvested in the summer. They seemed to be cut open by the plow, exposed and bleeding brown-black blood. Soon to be covered and soothed.

Down in the valley, a car created a tube of dust which floated intact across the fields. A little further away, the whole western horizon was a dark mass racing like a wave toward me. I felt like running back to the house, but I could not move. A dark veil slid up the valley. It soon passed me, dimming everything, sapping the colour from everything in its path. I turned to face the wind and waited.

Almost imperceptibly it began. One tiny flake landed on my ear. The wind began to blow. Another flake slammed into my cheek. And *another. I don't know how long I stood there but the wind had eased up and the snow was falling heavily when I regained my wits.*

Already a thin skiff of snow white covered the ground. Good. Very good, I thought. Sleep, fields, sleep. You deserve your rest. I walked softly, sometimes tiptoeing back to the house.

||||||||||||||||||||||||||||||||

Winter was mostly a fun time. You watched the giant snow blowers on the highway or the neighbour blowing out your driveway. Snowmobiles were everywhere. You didn't go by car if you could go by snowmobile to the store or over to a neighbour's farm. You longed to be out under the stars and moon, bounding over fluffy sparkling snow spray through winter wonderland scenery. Damn noisy things, though. But you could tell who was going where by the unique buzzing of their particular machine. Since you were dressed for the cold, you could just as easily stay outside, light the outdoor barbecue, or light a fire and roast hot dogs, boil up hot chocolate, and tell stories or joke around in the snow.

A farming community, as it is called, is a community. Although strung out along dirt roads, people know each other, they borrow equipment from each other or hire each other out to do this and that. Drive a tractor, drive a baler. Hire the kids to pick fruit. Rent your fields to someone. Buy your grain or hay from someone. Decorate your tractor and manure spreader for the annual village parade.

My parents enjoyed this new sense of community. The Barrie neighbourhood they moved out of had not been memorable for them either. At their lonely farm, they probably met and really got to know more interesting people than anywhere else they had lived. They developed lifelong friendships.

My younger brothers adapted well to their new lifestyle. From having to tear apart every motor on the farm at one time or another, Gary, my middle brother developed a love for motor mechanics and has been a Class A mechanic all his life. Greg, my youngest brother was more taken by the electronics, and he has been an equipment technician ever since.

My poor parents never did totally adapt to farming, mostly because my father still had to work a full-time job and work the farm. After eight years, they packed it in and headed back to London, Ontario, where all our moving had started. They bought a house on Wortley Road and lived there until they died. My two brothers now live north of Barrie.

If you like hard work and interesting animals, I recommend a farmhouse for you. If you've never lived in one, you don't know what you're missing. If you have lived in one, you are laughing now.

CHAPTER NINE

A Student's Life

Peterborough, Ontario

The first place I lived in Peterborough wasn't a house at all. It was the new Champlain College residence on the two-year-old Trent University campus on the banks of the Ottonabee River. The cement was still drying when I moved in.

Cement stairs, halls, walls, floors and ceilings. Was I supposed to be a monk or a prisoner? Surely this was not a student residence, I thought. How cruel to have come to this. I learned that Trent was modeled after Oxford and Cambridge and their stone masonry buildings and residences. A learned person needed the feeling of permanence, of history. A fine dream I thought, so long as you don't have to smell the cement drying.

The room was spartan. The furniture was teak: a desk with a small window in front; a bed; a wardrobe and a few drawers to house your sweaters and underwear. Washrooms and showers were down the hall. The first thing to alarm a teenage male was that there was no food in the residence. No fridge. No kitchen with full cupboards to hang out in. Meals were served up at precise times in the Great Hall. Great, I thought, as my stomach churned for something to eat.

Once again, I found myself surrounded by strangers in a strange place. But my compassionate Barrie high school teachers were right. This was a much friendlier place than high school. Someone, called the "don," had taken the time to review all the applicants and had placed us in our rooms according to a master plan. I'm not sure what all the criteria might have been, but on one floor and in one section you found a few students from each of first, second, and third year, some who had very different backgrounds from your own and some who were much like you. To their credit, the dons also assigned one second- or third-year student the task of introducing us to each other as we arrived. Sherry was poured and talk began.

In a situation like this, the first thing you try to do is find common ground—who plays cards? Who plays guitar and sings? Who smokes? Who knows where we can find some food? Before long, your circle of friends is formed in residence, and you have an even wider circle among those with whom you attend class. A social life arises instantaneously.

Our residence area was full of talented people, some of whom would become well known before too long. Playing guitar on the banks of the river, I found myself surrounded by Stan Rogers, Nigel Russel, Ian Tamblyn, Stephen Stone, Christopher Ward, and others who would later make names for themselves in the music business. Other students would become noted academics, lawyers, social workers, police officers, doctors or writers. The stimulation provided by just the students was more than the professors offered. That is part of the social plan of a university and of living in residence. Too bad they don't give degrees in Living in Residence. They would be equally as valuable as undergraduate degrees.

I liked living in residence for the camaraderie, but there were other things that got to me eventually. The lack of privacy. Every date you had you had to talk about, justify. Every party you felt you had to attend or risk being seen as anti-social. Every time you got hungry, you had to find something to eat, somehow. The food service contractors were more intent on making profits than filling our bellies. Servings were small and the food was icky at best. For a while, every night about 9 or 10, we would send out someone who had a car to the local A&W to order teen burgers and fries. When we ran out of money for that, we became most desperate. We found a student in the next building who could pick locks. Down to the kitchen we would sneak, pick the locks on the doors and refrigerators, and load up on food. After a few weeks of that, the food service started offering seconds at mealtimes. More icky food was better than nothing, and it did reduce the midnight raids.

In the end, I think it was the food, or lack thereof, that made me want to leave residence and try living in an apartment. It promised to be cheaper, as well, even if I did have a steak appetite. A good number of us made the same decision. On our last night at residence, a group of us climbed the small drumlin behind the campus and sat for hours looking down on our residence, reliving all our experiences there and knowing that that life was coming to an end. With our minds full and our stomachs empty, we turned to apartment living the next fall.

As a poor university student, my search for my very first cheap apartment was rewarded with a great bargain—a two-bedroom apartment for eighty dollars a month. Even in the late sixties, that was a hell of a deal. I shared it with a fellow I hardly knew and had little in common with except that we had the same household standards and an eye for a real deal. Since it was our first apartment, it was where we learned that you get what you pay for.

Bright sky blue was the colour of the outside of the house—topped by a dandy, shiny aluminum roof. It was very easy to see from a distance. On a windy day, you could also spot the myriad propellers, fans, and whirligigs gyrating away on the lawns. The squirrels that lived in the walnut tree above the house found the aluminum roof particularly appealing. Of course, they bounced and rolled walnuts all over it. But it was even more fun just to play on. Run and slide. Climb and skitter. It was only quiet up there in the dead of winter. Inside, it was never quiet.

We first noticed that sound traveled effortlessly between the two bedrooms and from the bathroom—through the walls separating them. It wasn't until we started putting up a few pictures that we realized why. Picture hanging nails didn't seem to hit anything solid—like, not even plaster. And the wall moved considerably with every tap of the hammer.

Honestly, have you ever encountered walls made of cardboard? Two layers thick for more stability and well-covered with wallpaper everywhere. The whole top of the house had been partitioned with large cardboard boxes, structurally supported by the few door jambs and a few studs at corners and joins. That's correct. No stud wall. Just cardboard attached, somehow, floor to ceiling. It was well done, mind you. We didn't catch on for at least a few days. The only thing we could think to do about it was add another layer of what we felt was strong and acoustically deadening wallpaper.

You really have to wonder about someone who would do such a thing, don't you? The cardboard walls, I mean. And of course, the lawn ornaments were all home-handyman-made, as was much of the lawn furniture. The landlord and landlady lived downstairs amid their TV tables, plaids, crocheted throws, and lazy boy chairs. They watched TV from morning to night, going out occasionally to shop or tend to things outside in the yard. Both he and his wife were perfectly happy with his handywork. Proud of it, in fact. And they were also perfectly happy in general. That should teach us something, shouldn't it?

Although our apartment was supposed to be "self-contained," it was simply at the top to the stairs with no door to it. Like it or not, we got TV all day and into the night. And whatever they were cooking. Tuna casserole. Meatloaf. Liver and onions. You know, smells that really stick to the walls until morning.

The next year I moved into a house down and across the street. It was brick, and very solid and quiet inside. From the street-side window, I could still see the old blue house down the street. It sure had character. And I hardly remember a thing about living in the brick place for a year.

||||||||||||||||||||||||||||||

CHAPTER TEN

Living Together

Two Peterborough, Ontario "Communal Houses"

Somehow or another, after sharing an apartment with only one other person, I moved on to sharing with two others, then three and five and six and... Why? I don't know. Safety in numbers, maybe. As young twenty-somethings, it seemed to take about a half-dozen of us to muster the skills of one together and responsible adult. Most of us were in love, "living together" for the first time and starting new jobs after finishing university. Talk about your stress factors.

The houses where we lived en masse were older brick buildings. Fleming Place was a stately, modest mansion—beautiful wood paneling, staircases, high ceilings, marble fireplace, and so on. It was old, but the grandeur and the five bedrooms remained. I can't remember why we moved, but most of us who lived at Fleming Place moved one street back to a duplex that was as big but not nearly as nice as Fleming Place. We spent about a year in each house.

For those of you who have never lived with six or eight other unrelated people in a big house, I have this advice: don't even think about it. Sure, it's a great idea for cutting your rent costs and never being lonely, but that's about all it has going for it. Having lots of friends is a good thing, but trying to live successfully with all of them is another matter. You can *lose* a lot of friends that way.

When you get right down to the nitty-gritty of daily living, people are different. Some put the cap back on the toothpaste, some don't. Some people stink; some don't. Some people can cook; some can't. Some people know how to find dirt and clean it, some don't. Some people have surprising traits, others don't.

I can't remember who all lived in the different houses, but the main ones were Rob who I had shared a previous apartment with, his girlfriend, Cynthia, and Rob's mother, who had suffered a nervous breakdown and was now lying in bed recovering from it with cigarettes, beer, and anti-depressants sent by mail by her doctor. There was Chris, a budding musician and all-night local rock DJ and sudden vegetarian, Zeke, another musician fellow with a one-track music mind, and Lex, the twenty-year-old with the granny look.

She was interesting. By a quirk of anatomical fate, Lex became transformed by hippy dresses and round wire-framed glasses into a perfect little old lady figure. And she lived it to the hilt, complete with mannerisms, little old lady voice and petit point stitchery with her at all times. Her mission that year, as it turned out, was to find nice, virginal young men and teach them a thing or three about making love to a woman. It was her contribution to the growing women's movement, she said.

Kate, my wife now, had just left her middle-class home and moved in with me. We even rolled out the red carpet for her when she arrived. Really. Not exactly a wedding or anything, but a funny, folksy celebration of breaking free and all that. I had finished a degree in anthropology and was looking around for work, though I didn't have much direction at the time. We were all growing our hair and drifting into being hippies. Love, peace, drugs, and rock and roll. We had it all. Or at least some did; some didn't. But we all looked the part.

So, there we all are, and we've called a house meeting, and everyone is there more or less. There's the serious musician, actually awake in the daylight hours today, who finds the regular world slightly out of reach—especially his phone bills. Rob and his girlfriend, Cynthia, can hardly leave each other alone, every minute being devoted to foreplay of one kind or another. Lexa, the granny girl, has brought along her petit point to keep her hands busy. Chris, the all-night DJ and budding singer-songwriter, is still trying to convince everyone of vegetarianism, peace, harmony, and rock and roll. And two more who had dropped acid a while back and are now fixated on the paisley designs on my shirt more so than the meeting. Mrs. E. stays in bed. And then there's Kate and me, and we think we're normal—right. Living with a group like this?!

Well, just try having a meeting of this group to work out the household duties—cooking dinner, shopping for food and supplies, cleaning the bathroom, mowing the lawns or shovelling snow, and so on. The vegetarian says he won't do dinner if there's meat. Those without cars don't want to do the grocery shopping. The lovebirds want to know if things like Kleenex are personal or household items. The two acid heads can't face cleaning bathrooms at the moment. The musician and the all-night DJ claim special status because they work at night and need to sleep undisturbed in the morning. Everyone wants to work out what's equal—like one dinner-cooking equals one lawn-mow or one bathroom-clean equals two doing-the-dishes. If they never get any phone calls, why should they have to pay a share for the phone? And so it goes.

Soon we discovered that the ideals of communal, cooperative living through consensus decision-making were out of our reach. Far out of our reach. Maybe some semblance of peaceful coexistence can be had with a group of people who were very similar to begin with. Eight people who are radically different do not a group make.

For most of us, this was our first opportunity to have our tolerance levels tested. Some people had very few life skills—like knowing how to shop, to clean bathrooms or cook. Their mommies made sure of that. We tried to convince some of these folks to bring their mommies with them if they couldn't do their blasted chores properly! So, the greatest burdens fell, as usual, on those who already knew how to do the chores properly. A few people in living situations like these manage to avoid their chores for months before the rest of the house has the courage to kick them out. And then they don't pay their bills, either.

It was a year of spinning in the wind. Not only was life in the house always a challenge from a cooperative point of view, but everyone had their personal crises, their radical shifts from university to a career or job, or mates coming and going. People moved in; people moved out. After you have lived like this for a while, you have no need to watch soap operas. Seen it all before.

CHAPTER ELEVEN

The End of the Road

Boulter, Ontario

Deciding to leave the womb of our university city, Peterborough, and to do the back-to-the-land thing, my new and forever partner, Kate, and I headed north in search of a farm. In a lonely country store inquiring about places to rent, a customer overheard us and made us an offer. The farmhouse needed a lot of work, and if we would do it, he'd provide the supplies—and free rent. Except for paying *us* to live somewhere, this was as cheap as the rent was going to get. We drove on another ten kilometres or so to the farm.

Fortunately for the self-conscious pair we were, you couldn't see the house from the road. It was a shabby, grey insulbrick box with a steep, pointed roof and a squat front with a low, closed-in veranda. Most windows were uniformly covered with tattered bits of plastic that had been last year's storm windows. One could see that every attempt at construction and maintenance had been feeble. We hadn't driven around this particular area before, but we would soon learn that our farmhouse was no better and no worse than all the others.

Futility hung in the air like a fog. There was nothing of quality anywhere to be seen. Run-down houses, run-down barns, run-down machinery, run-down vehicles, run-down stores, run-down people. Some say that Al Capp's Dogpatch was partly (or perhaps *could have been*) based on life in this area. Whatever it was that people had tried to do here never quite worked out. There were a few success stories, mostly of the human spirit type, not the material.

Originally cleared and settled around the turn of the century, the timber sales were probably the first and las source of riches for the settlers. Boulter is about 80 kilometres south of Algonquin Park and about 160 kilometres north of the last of the good farmland and reasonable temperatures. There may have been a few good years of farming when prices were good and the weather unusually good, but after a few decades, most people gave up farming altogether.

By the 1960s, the area had been designated a forest renewal zone, and people were paid to plant trees on their scrabbly farms. And they did. What they also needed was money to replant themselves somewhere else, but that never came.

Back in the 1950s, uranium was mined nearby. Many of the men from around here went to work at the mine. It, too, proved unprofitable and closed a decade later, leaving behind the usual legacy of radioactive waste and tailings, and ex-miners. Many of the older men had worked in logging operations nearby, but the timber was all gone now. Almost everyone was unemployed. The few exceptions were teachers, postal workers, county road crewmen, and a few clergy. About fifteen jobs in all.

We had a small, mostly Labrador female dog we called Ruba. Suckers for dogs that we were, we soon acquired a tired old Afghan hound needing "a place to run." By late winter, another friend of ours had dropped off his Newfoundland mother and her five-month-old pup while he went away somewhere.

The dogs got along quite well despite their differences. Prune, the Newfoundland mother, was immense in her black winter coat. Her smaller ball of black fur was named Amanita. Newfoundland dogs run up to 170 pounds and stand almost a metre tall at the shoulder. Not lap dogs. Caesar, the blond Afghan, was regal indeed, his tail perfectly curled over his back. But he was as dumb as a bag of hammers. Though roughly the same dimensions as the Newfie, the Afghan weighed about a third as much and would blow away in a stiff wind. Ruba was smarter than all of them put together, and even though she was the smallest, she was the leader.

Country folk always enquire about your dogs. What are they for?

I had trained Ruba how to hunt groundhogs because we were so poor we could barely afford to feed ourselves. In turn, she was training the other dogs in that fine art. Early one winter morning, the four of them had made it to a neighbour's farm and cornered something under their well-house. We often had Ruba in the truck with us when we traveled about, and the woman of the house had met Ruba a few times and recognized her.

Kate answered the phone call from the neighbour. She grinned from ear to ear.

"Did you know that your dog Ruba was running with a mother black bear and her cub? And there's something with them that looks like a brown monkey!"

Few people in these parts knew what pedigree dogs looked like. Theirs were all mongrels of the tire-biting, farm dog variety. Of course, as the story spread, we were asked of what use these kinds of dogs were. In this eke-out-a-living place, everyone had to pull their weight somehow, including the dogs. We had a few answers which seemed to both please and perplex the askers.

We had to cut our winter wood in the maple and ironwood forest that fanned out from our long road. And we had to do it in the late winter, because we were quickly running out of wood, our only source of heat. Getting the wood out through the deep and heavy snow and back to the house was not an easy task. Back to the land we had gone, forgetting that it would be covered with snow much of the year.

After cobbling together a large and rugged sleigh using a pair of old skis as runners, we harnessed Prune, the Newfoundland, to it. Prune's owner had had the forethought to have a harness specially made but had never used it. With very little training, Prune soon loved to pull the sleigh. She had no idea where she was to pull the sleigh to, however. That's where Ruba came in. She led Prune with a leash and coaxed her on from the front while I handled steering the rear. Prune pulled loads of cord wood many times her own weight and delighted in it. Her steamy panting hung in the air like puffs of smoke from an old iron horse. When I stopped to rest, she wondered what the heck I was doing. *Pull, pull, pull* was all she wanted to do.

Caesar was considerably less useful. As a guard dog, he did OK because of his size, and because he was almost blind, he barked at everyone, including us. He did teach us one more thing about the Newfoundland breed one afternoon. We were taking the dogs for a walk along a wide river in the winter. The ice was thick and clear along the banks, but the middle of the river was still open and flowing with black water. Being blind and stupid, Caesar followed his nose for a nice drink of fresh water and fell through the ice. And there was no way he could climb out.

We scrambled up and down the riverbank looking for long poles or vines or… but that was utterly futile. Our hearts sank as we watched Caesar about to sink. By this time, Prune had seen the trouble that Caesar was in. On sheer instinct, she flattened herself over the ice and made her way out to where Caesar was trying to cling to the ice. Prune went through the thin ice just in front of Caesar, who miraculously seized the opportunity and climbed out over her back and onto more solid ice. He was safe, and now Prune was in the river.

Prune smashed her front paws on the ice in front of her until it would break no more, and then she slopped her paws on the ice and lay there. She looked absolutely pathetic. As if she wished she hadn't done what she just did. That hang-dog look.

Thinking she was tired or hypothermic, we were sure she would slip away in minutes. We winced, almost unable to watch as she sank back in the water a ways. But then she leaped clean out and onto the ice. Again, she flattened herself out and scrambled to shore. We realized that she had been letting her paws freeze to the ice so she could haul herself out. After shaking herself, she was hardly wet at all. And very happy.

If ever you find yourself fishing among icebergs, as Newfies do, you'll want to have a Newfoundland dog on board. They earn their keep.

Ruba's accolades came as leader of the groundhog patrol. It took a lot to feed four big dogs, and the neighbours were thankful for the culling of the local population. There weren't many dogs that could successfully hunt groundhogs. Ruba had the knack—sit on the backside of a hole, downwind from the entrance, and freeze. For hours, if necessary. Eventually, the groundhog came out of its hole far enough that Ruba could catch it in one leap. Even Prune and Amanita learned the technique, though the speed of their pounces left much to be desired. The question the locals had about how the dogs earned their keep was answered. Now, what about us? What did we do?

For generations, people had moved *away* from this area. No one had moved *to* it in a long time, except for schoolteachers because they had to. So just what was it that we thought we could be doing here to earn a living? Or were we just hippies on welfare? People never put it quite that way, but we knew what they meant. We must have been crazy or worse.

Arriving in July, it was too late to plant any kind of cash crop. The farm machinery at our farm was 1930s vintage—a modified Model T of a tiny dumpster truck and a decrepit tractor that ran much faster downhill than uphill. The gravelly land hadn't been plowed in years, and sod had cemented over the fields. So, yes, we did have to look for work after all.

A few other crazy people had recently moved to the area, and we soon found each other. One couple with two school-aged kids lived not far from our place. Another couple with a teenage daughter lived much further away. After just a couple of get-togethers, we learned that we shared the same problem. We had no idea what we were thinking when we decided to move up here. None of us anticipated the bleak job outlook. Young fools that we were.

The couple with the two kids had been dismayed at the lack of extra-curricular activities or cultural content at the local school. The principal was sympathetic but was saddled with only a few staff, who had no extras to offer. For sixty kilometres in any direction, there were no music teachers, no choirs, no theatre groups, no active community groups of any kind, and no community hall. Culturally and artistically, this area had been dead for decades.

Culture. Among us we had a theatre arts, dance, and sewing talent, one with woodworking and shop skills, and two music teachers, Kate and myself. We were all university-educated and gung-ho. We could bring culture and arts to the school! In two days, we had concocted a government grant application to fill what we felt were some big gaps in the school and the area. The school was supportive.

Within six weeks, we had the grant and went to work in the local elementary school. Those in the school seemed happy to have us around. We did remedial work with slower students, started music programs and sewing, wood-working and theatre classes. The kids loved it. Several of them were particularly pleased to be learning guitar or harmonica or piano. For the most part, these students were not good at the academic curriculum, but they could shine musically. Perhaps for the first time in their lives, there was something they could do and be proud of. We found that many of the kids we were working with came from large, poor families that lived in two- and three-room, dirt-floored cabins.

We visited a few of their cabins when dropping kids off from music classes after school. Eight or ten kids, the last few of them were progressively more mentally handicapped than early ones. Evidence of drinking everywhere. Beer cases piled high. Garbage piled high. Old cars piled high. Bruises on the wife, and kids piled high. Despair piled high. An assault to every sense we had, these more-than-humble homes seemed to exist in a Dickensian dimension we could never have imagined. Brutal living in every way possible. We really hoped that we could at least bring them the joy of music, dance, and art.

Many parents were thankful for the new enrichment activities and the vibrant life at the school. Many parents did not appreciate it at all, which we were completely unaware of. We would soon find out.

Within two months, a revolt was brewing, and the school held a public meeting to clear the air. We were shocked to find that a fair number of parents had had a bit to drink before coming, and they were loud and seething. Little did we know what lay ahead that evening.

The principal explained the things we were doing in the school: how many children we were giving extra help to; how many students were taking music lessons; how many were involved in dance, the theatre club, and so on.

This only made the crowd more restless, and several loud men stood up and called down the principal. "WE WANT TO SPEAK! LET THE PARENTS SPEAK!"

Ignoring all the work we were doing in the school, the chief complaints were two-fold. From the more religious came the observation that we were a very poor moral example to their children. "After all, the women have different last names than the men, but they are all living together, aren't they? The kids can figure that out. They're living in sin."

The largest group, however, had a real hatred for us because we had stolen work from them. We were mystified by that comment. But the explanation was coming. One father who had a son who really enjoyed what we were doing in the school, stood up, waving his arms about.

"Just how is it that all you artsy newcomers come here and get government handouts to teach this useless cultural crap to our kids?! We don't need that. What we need is work for the men who have lived here all their lives. They've got families to raise, eh! If there's any government grant money coming here, we men should get it. We could be out cutting brush or working on roads. *We* should have the jobs. Not these hippies. We need to talk to our politicians! This should be *our* money!"

Many other men agreed loudly. I don't recall how quickly we tried to get out of that meeting, but I can't remember exactly how it ended. The principal called the next day to say that we would have to leave because of all the flack. Another school in a larger town twenty-five kilometres away took on the women of our group, and the grant, and did so gladly. There would be no "living in sin" connections made, and the parents of the school were happy to have them. We guys lost out.

So did the angry, out-of-work men who never did find road or bush work or more government handouts than they were already getting to stay drunk. Most of them probably couldn't read or write, let alone apply for grants or cutting permits in the bush. And things returned to normal at the school, too.

||||||||||||||||||||||||||||||||

Remnants of a small Mennonite community could be found in the vicinity whenever you saw a well-run farm. The farmhouses were huge. A few large families clung to more traditional ways and dress. Garbed from head to toe, the girls were given womanly tasks like cooking and cleaning. Guys wore black and did guy stuff, like farming with horses and threshing by hand. The guys ate first, and then the women folk. Never together. They kept to themselves. So self-sufficient were they that unless you went to see *them*, it was as if they didn't exist. We never saw them anywhere else.

We saw what an "intentional community" could do and be, and what it couldn't. With hard work and more hard work, you could get by on this poor farmland. But that's all. The elders said the community continued to crumble because there were just too few left. Half the young people just left. Most were curious about life outside of their insular religious community. They didn't come back.

I've often wondered why God would drag his followers to such a marginal farming area when there was plenty of good land to be had further south. Why not leave this land to the wicked or the wayward? They'd have had plenty of company here. I think that the Mennonites' work ethic kept them in place. Why move when you had all this work to do? It was an honest life, free of material wealth. That is how they framed it.

|||||||||||||||||||||||||||||||||

Kate had a similar spirit to the Mennonites and to Prune when it came to hard work. She decided she would learn how to use a chainsaw and help with the woodcutting in winter. Once she had bucked up a few dozen pieces, she would want it all hauled in that day. No matter how tired you or she might be, the wood had to come in. For a first-time faller and bucker, Kate was getting to be quite good with a chainsaw. For the first few days, she was unable to put the chainsaw down after working with it for a while. Having been told how important it was to always have a firm grip on the saw; such was her grasp that her fingers welded themselves to the grip. I would have to come over to her and pry her hands off the chainsaw, one aching finger at a time.

At Easter that year, my youngest brother, Greg, came for a visit. He was thirteen and had just gone through the big growth spurt of swaggering male adolescence. He'd even been pumping iron and showed off his bulging biceps. Kate had big biceps of her own and gave Greg a taunting flex of her arm. Teasing her that *her* muscles wouldn't be hard and strong like a guy's, he challenged her to arm-wrestle. She obliged and buried Greg's knuckles into the table in a second. With her left arm, too. Even when Greg was ready that time. Greg had a lot more respect for "girl" muscles after that.

Indeed, we had both toughened up considerably over the past year and learned more hard lessons than we cared to think about.

Kate and I had hoped that when we moved up here, we would finally be together, just the two of us. We had always shared large houses with others and needed some time for us. You would think that renting a farmhouse at the end of everywhere would be the perfect place for solitude. It didn't work out that way.

Our first problem was that the two men who had been living in the farmhouse, as rent-free caretakers, had not moved when they were supposed to have. The very thought of moving had sent them into a month-long drinking binge from which they had not recovered. No such thing as tenant rights up here. The landlord had asked them to move out, and that was that. We could see why he wanted them gone. One was a rather nice old chap who needed much help and care, which was being provided by a middle-aged fellow who helped him drink his old age pension check away every month in this rent-free house. They had a good thing going.

Arriving with all our stuff, we simply had to move in anyway. After a few weeks, we finally convinced them to start making some calls and taking their drinking party somewhere else. Unfortunately, they had to split up. The old guy went south to a relative's place, and the younger one went north. We felt bad, but it wasn't our problem.

Just when we thought we had the place to ourselves, the landlord and his lady-friend would show up for the weekend. That was part of the deal. He could come up and stay every once in a while, because he had to haul building materials a day's drive up from Toronto where he lived and worked. Of course, he'd do a little fishing or hunting before heading back in a day or two.

In the end, the no-rent deal never worked out. The landlord didn't come through with any materials, and so we couldn't do the work he expected in lieu of rent. And he drank a lot, too. This truly was an end-of-the-road frame job.

Every few months, someone would arrive on our doorstep in need of shelter—physical or emotional. One of the newcomer couples broke up, and the husband came to live with us. The fellow with the Newfoundland dogs also had a break-up. He left fairly soon after but left us with the dogs until he found another place for them.

One more acquaintance simply got marooned there after dropping in for a brief visit as a snowstorm hit. He had to stay for two weeks until we dug ourselves out of mammoth drifts across our quarter mile of driveway. On some days we would almost get it all plowed out before something on the Jeep broke. Then the drive would drift in again overnight. Or the temperature would drop into the minus-forties, and we couldn't get the Jeep to start. When we were working, we had to hike up and over a ten-acre windswept snowfield to get to the county road where a co-worker would pick us up. Damn near froze to death out there.

By spring, we felt like we had put in the longest year of our lives. Except for making friends with the two other newcomer families, we only had two other "local" friends. One was an older couple with whom we traded our eggs for milk. Actually, all we got was the skimmed milk, from which we made cottage cheese and a bit of cream to go with it. The fellow had been the county snow-plow driver in winter, the grader in summer. They ran a modest mixed farm but survived mainly on their pensions.

The other couple had happily found each other long ago. They were misfits, too. Iva was huge. She wasn't really fat, just built like a centre in football. Growing up in an area completely devoid of iodine in the soil had affected her thyroid, and she had many symptoms of gigantism. She was not pretty in any way, but she was a beautiful person who could make beautiful things. You wished you could turn her inside out. Her hands were bulky, easily twice the size of mine. Yet from those hands came the finest sewing, crocheting, and tatting you'd ever see.

Tatting was new to us. Basically, you start with thin white string and end up with elegant doilies by tying a thousand knots and loops with it. To see those immense fingers busily tying tiny knots as we talked over coffee was like watching a miracle unfold. It seemed so impossible.

Craig, her husband, was an orphan in England. As a boy of eight, he was essentially sold by the orphanage and adopted by a family in the area in the 1930s. They quickly put him to work on their farm so that their oldest son could stay in school. Craig never made it to school. Never learned to read or write. But he was a good woodsman and keen gardener. Even at seventy, Craig had the finest stacks of cord wood and the neatest vegetable garden around.

Like many others up here, he had married someone who lived only a few side roads away. Iva had worked as the county clerk while Craig worked in logging and tended the farm. In spite of the harshness of their upbringing, the harshness of their lives, and the harshness of their neighbours, they were gentle, wise, and warm.

Iva taught Kate the fine art of quilt-making. Kate was a quick study and began sewing some truly lovely quilt tops. A ladies' church group that Iva belonged to did the final quilting—where the hand-stitching all over the quilt binds together the top and bottom with the batten in the middle. Stitches should be evenly spaced, evenly tight, and wisely designed to hold the quilt together so that it lies perfectly flat, it puffs up where it should and doesn't where it shouldn't. A quilting bee of women has to agree on all that as they each work on their side or end of the quilt mounted on a frame to stretch it taught. This bee was as good as they get.

Kate never mastered the quilting part, but she sewed fine tops. For several years after we moved on to Québec, Kate would send quilt-tops to Iva for the final quilting. They made for fine Christmas presents and a handy extra income. Some would sell for up to six hundred dollars. Remember this is the 1970s—so you can imagine the quality of quilts Kate and Iva's quilting bee was making.

These were the people we missed the most when we left. I guess they could see that we were misfits, too. And we did have much in common with them, even though we were separated by forty years in age and about a third of a metre in hair length.

Although we had encountered more despair and cussedness here than we had ever imagined, we had also found decency and goodness. Both were locally grown. What is it exactly that makes some poor families happy and successful and others miserable and dejected? The happier ones went to church and had a certain faith about life. Perhaps their upbringing had not included drunken fathers in their homes. Perhaps basic literacy had something to do with it. Perhaps, taken together, these factors helped some people rise above where others sank below.

After about eight months of driving around the area, we found that all the county roads except two came to dead ends. One was a gravel forest service road that eventually connected to a highway eighty kilometres to the north. The other went south and connected to a highway about six kilometres away. Every other road simply petered out into an old logging road or a one-time pasture that had since been planted with pines. Indeed, almost everything here was a dead end.

Even we soon found our dead ends. Our futures were not there. Kate had only finished first year university and had taken two years off to work out what she really wanted to study. She had been in general arts, where she excelled but she couldn't see where she should be going. After doing music with young children in the schools, she realized that that was what she wanted to do with her life. (And it is what she does to this day.) So we had to find a university with the program she was looking for. And away we went, away from the dead ends.

If your life is framed by dead ends, you either wither and die there or decide to move on. We still had the will and spirit to do that. I only wish we had been able to leave some of that behind for others to draw upon.

Now, almost fifty years later, I think about the withering death of so many small communities of people in Canada over that period. The family farm and thousands of farming communities from coast to coast, the East Coast fishing villages, forestry and mining towns. So many wrenching and painful decisions being made by good people to leave behind a lifestyle that is no longer economically viable. The pain of staying might be worse, but that is no consolation.

CHAPTER TWELVE

Retreats

Paudash Lake

Near the end of June, we moved only an hour's drive south of Boulter, Ontario, to my wife's family cottage at Paudash Lake. It soon proved to be much farther away than that.

We stayed there maybe six weeks, but it was the refresher we needed. In June, there were no other cottagers around. Quiet except for the birds and squirrels, there was a beautiful solitude to being the only people on a sparkling lake. The family cottage was small, a kitchen and living room across the front and three tiny bedrooms and a bathroom across the back. On the front deck, you looked out under tall pines to a rocky shore and Paudash Lake in all directions. It was Group of Seven country.

It was comforting to be back in a cottage again after so many years. To see the cockeyed, owner-built shelves and cupboards. To hear and watch waves lapping the shore. To smell pines. To feel sand underfoot. To understand the meaning of retreat.

Precisely three hours after school let out for the summer, what had been a ghost town sprang to life as carload after laden carload rolled into the other cottages along the road. Kids sprang out and climbed over everything. Parents lugged gear. Dogs barked. Outboard motors fired up. Boats and skiers carved across the lake. Chainsaws howled. Circular saws buzzed. Hammers whacked.

Neighbours who had not seen each other for ten months visited with each other. Kids ran to greet other kids as they arrived. Here, everyone was really friendly. A spirited community had popped up overnight. And there were no dead-enders here. The woman next door was on her way to becoming a well-known Ontario watercolourist. Two boys in the next cottage over would become doctors. And so it went through the neighbourhood. People talked of their dreams, not their troubles.

With such inspiration all around us, we found the courage to seek our own dreams once again. We took a fruitless trip to Ottawa to investigate a music program for my wife. But we did learn of another one in Québec City, at Laval University. We visited there, too, and decided that we would move before the summer was over.

Leaving the cottage was difficult. It held so many memories for my wife. Places that you grow up in are like that. Part of you is in them. Part of them in you.

Having a retreat or going on one is something worth considering. It is a place where the frames of your other life are removed. Sometimes you need that.

CHAPTER THIRTEEN

The Golden Rule

La Vieille Maison de Rang St. Jean,
St. Bernard de Dorchester, Québec

Having expectations is often a hindrance. If you set your expectations too high or completely off the mark, people or circumstances will never live up to them, and you'll be disappointed. If you set them too low, you may be pleasantly surprised. If you simply approach things without expectations, you stand a far better chance of discovering just what is.

The way to finding a house to rent in rural Québec in the early 1970s came as a complete surprise to us. My wife and I had traveled to Québec City because she was about to start a Bachelor of Music program at Laval University. We had left staid, English Ontario behind and ventured deep into the heart of old, rural Québec. Time to learn French, we declared to ourselves.

We were kind of grow-your-own, back-to-the-land types who had a dog and liked country places—and found them much cheaper to rent than a city house. Having drawn a circle with a forty-kilometre radius around Québec City, we were camping and driving about, looking for houses to rent. All the places advertised in papers were in towns and villages. We were sure we had seen many empty places on the side roads, but no "For Rent" or "For Sale" signs on them. And none advertised.

When we finally made enough sense describing our problem in our broken French to a general store clerk, he and his wife painstakingly tried to make it clear to us that we had to visit the curé—the village priest. We couldn't see the connection, but we obliged anyway. We were sure we had been misunderstood yet again.

The curé, a quiet and confident man, was most interested to talk with us. He asked us all kinds of questions about who we were, what we did, what brought us here, and all that. Lots of pleasantries. We tried not to appear too daft but gently asked if he could offer any advice on finding a country house to rent. Well, he said, he would try to help. He'd talk about it in church on Sunday and we could call back on Monday. So, we did. Heck, what did we know? We weren't Catholic.

On Monday morning, we were given a list of places to look at and wished providence and God's blessing by the curé.

The first place wasn't very nice at all, but the second one wasn't too bad—at least someone was living in it and it looked somewhat cared for. The negotiation over rental price and availability was a great comedy routine. We had no common language. I had lived in Montréal earlier in my life and had a good ear for hearing and understanding French. Kate had more formal training, and had been to France for a while, so she could speak 'real' French a bit. Lorenzo and his wife Marie-Ange, the landlords, did not speak French as we knew it. Indeed, many Québecois would have trouble understanding them. They spoke Beauceron—that is, a regional and ancient dialect in La Beauce region south of Québec City. We weren't prepared for this.

Among the things we quickly learned was that the local accent and vocabulary in the Beauce region was over three hundred years old. With the profusion of modern radio and TV middle-of-the-road accents, the old ways were dying out, but the old folks still spoke a great twist on French. Also in those three hundred years, we were the first English people to come to live there. Being the local novelty was our ace in the hole. People were amused by us. Being almost unable to understand what was being said to us also amused them, I'm sure.

Seeing how poor we were, our landlords asked if twenty-five dollars a month would be too much for us to pay. Part of our problem was we were sure we had misunderstood, and he really meant a hundred and twenty-five a month. After writing it down, we realized that we had a gift from heaven (via the local curé) and said, yes, we could manage that.

Our landlords, both in their fifties or sixties, were stout and stooped and always smelled of pig manure, or chicken manure, or cow manure. Take your pick, if you can tell the difference. They were much nicer than they smelled.

When we arrived with our U-Haul trailer filled with our meagre belongings, people from up and down the road came to help unload. We weren't sure if it was neighbourliness or curiosity, but they were all there, pitching in. As we came to the last few items in the trailer, looks of consternation spread across their faces and much conversation ensued.

"Where is your bed?" they worried. In this cardboard box, we told them in our French.

Being one of the first people to own a waterbed, we soon realized that these people had never even heard of such a thing. Setting up the frame, we then asked for a garden hose and began to fill it up. At least four people crowded around the bedroom window to watch this procedure from start to finish. When it was over, we had to show them what it was like. I can't say that any of them liked the feeling of lying on a waterbed, but at least we were satisfied that they knew we had a bed.

When we awoke the next morning, there were two metal beds in the driveway. No one even bothered to say who gave them to us. Similarly, homemade pies would magically appear in our cupboards from time to time. Or a basket of fruit or vegetables. Now, a house that is over two hundred years old should have a lock or two, right? None. There had never been a lock on any of the doors that we could see. We decided to ask about this. My wife is particularly careful about returning favours or at least thanking the donors. When they snuck in while we were out, to plant things in our cupboards, Kate was dumbfounded. There were at least three families that could have perpetrated the act of kindness.

There were no locks because no stranger or burglar could get past all the houses on the road without being seen and dealt with. Everybody watched every movement. Having locks on your door would mean that you did not trust your neighbourhood or that you had things to hide from others or that you were afraid of somebody… There really was no good reason for a lock.

It helps to endear yourself to your new neighbours, which we were having a little trouble accomplishing. I hadn't planned on it, but by accident, I did. The young couple moving out of the house we were moving into were about to become parents for the first time. They were still moving out the day we moved in, and so we met, along with all the neighbours who were there to help out.

The mother-to-be was very heavy with child, as they say, and the neighbours were trying to be cheery by divining whether the baby would be a boy or girl by dangling a coin on a string over her tummy. If it turned one way, it would be a boy, the other way, a girl. It really helped who was holding the string and coin, because some people were known to be better diviners than others. We all had to take our turns.

Now, I had spent some time with sheep and noted how pregnant ewes looked. If they were carrying just one lamb, they hung low in the middle. If they were to have twins, they were so broad that they had trouble getting through the stall gates. I noticed that this young woman had the same carriage as the latter and indeed had trouble going through a door straight on. So, I said I thought she was going to have twins. That really made everyone laugh. I felt foolish, of course. And the coin on the string spun this way and that.

Two weeks later, she did have twins, a boy and a girl, much to everyone's surprise, including her doctor, I assume. However, I was soon king of the diviners for having nailed that one. Strings and coins appeared for me to try whenever there was a pregnant lass in the neighbourhood.

We had arrived in late summer, and by the end of September, we were getting concerned about our wood supply for the winter. I should have mentioned earlier that this old house hadn't been updated in about a century. There was a cookstove in the kitchen and a larger wood furnace in the dugout cellar. We did have the luxury of an indoor toilet, and there was a bathtub, but no hot water heater (we did get one a short while later)—you trucked buckets of water from the cookstove to the bathroom for a bath. At any rate, we needed wood soon, so I asked around where I could buy some cord wood or mill ends. Everyone I asked seemed surprised by the question, and no one had an answer.

My landlord, Lorenzo, figured out what the problem was. Everyone who lived there *owned* their land and had a woodlot that they managed for themselves. Many did maple syrup and their woodcutting at the same time—late winter when it was nice to work and there was still snow on the ground for the sleighs to move the wood out easily. Yes, most people still worked a few horses. It had only been for the previous seven years that the local roads had been plowed out all winter. Until just a few years before, people had used their horses, wagons, and sleighs (and skidoos) to get about in winter. He said my problem was twofold—I needed a woodlot, and I needed horses—and I needed to have had my cutting done last spring. He was right, of course.

A few days later, when we came home from university, the woodshed was full of wood. Lorenzo explained that all the neighbours had contributed a little from their own supplies and even the Duclos boys from up the road had done much of the stacking work. They were all very happy that we had our winter's wood, because now they wouldn't have to worry about us freezing to death. We were happy, too! Even though we tried our best to offer payment or work or something for this great gift, we were rebuffed. It seemed that there was much delight in having gotten the Duclos to do something productive. That was payment enough for everybody.

Madame Duclos, also stout and stooped, was a little hard of hearing, and when she spoke, she sounded like a bullhorn with lips. I believe she also thought we were hard of hearing because we asked her to repeat herself so often. She had a good handle on the Beauce accent, and dentures. Everyone over the age of nineteen had dentures. A high-sugar, low-hygiene regime for most Québecers produces the most dentured populace in Canada. So, we also had to cope with the clacking and tongue-slurring necessary to keep these dentures in place while they talked. Madame was most kind and jovial, but she did leave your ears ringing when she left. She also seemed very nosy to us, at first.

The Duclos house was easily as old and as un-modern as ours. It was about two hundred paces up the road on the other side. Like ours, it was built within about three metres of the edge of the road. Straight across from it was another house. You could play catch porch to porch between the two. Rural French-Canadians built their homes so close to the road for reasons that eluded English settlers, who put theirs at the end of long lanes. Being of one religion and culture, French-Canadians were more closely knit together. As they drove or walked by a house, they would stop and engage in conversation. From the inside perspective, you didn't have to drop what you were doing to chat—just fling open the door. In such an environment, your life was quite exposed.

We finally accepted the fact that what we thought was snoopiness on the part of our neighbours was not that at all. The only way that they could care for each other, look out for each other, was to know intimately what their needs might be. And rather than force people to ask for help or even to offer it, people just *gave* whatever seemed to be needed without much ado. We appeared to be quite needy, and this was a good thing for the Duclos. Until we came along, they were the neediest family on the road. That they could do something for us (wood-stacking, baking pies, giving us jams and veggies) lifted their spirits.

Unfortunately for the Duclos, it was the other kind of spirits that got them down. Their house had produced the veritable seventh son of the seventh son, but the supernatural abilities were sadly missing. The dad and a few of his adult sons who still lived at home drank ceaselessly. Poor Madame Duclos had lived her entire life surrounded by drunken bums. Mostly they were nice drunks, but drunks, nevertheless. People were most impressed when the sons sobered up enough to really do some work in getting us our wood. I think they surprised themselves, too. And Madame could smile in church on Sundays.

One of Lorenzo's sons, barely out of teenage-hood and just a farm kid with little education, told us a little about this giving and sharing that went on. He had asked his father why he rented the place so cheaply and why he gave us wood and even asked his sons to do some free work for us—plow our garden, fix the road, plow the drive in winter. Lorenzo told them he was teaching them about giving. And about the Golden Rule. How could we ever become part of the community unless we were treated like we were?

We also led interesting lives that were worlds apart from our neighbours' farming life. Whatever we had to tell them about, they were happy to listen. We were university-educated and undoubtedly a source of much amusement. Down on the farm, however, our neighbours were the well-educated ones. They knew how and when to grow garden plants and where the berry patches were and when to go smelt fishing. They could even make cough syrup from local bark and plants, though I wouldn't recommend it. My wife complained of a sore throat to our landlord's wife, whereupon she appeared with this bottle of dark liquid. She yanked open Kate's mouth, produced a huge swab and had a go at the back of Kate's throat before she knew what was happening! It did the job, I guess. Kate never complained of a sore throat again.

My second claim to fame among my neighbours had to do with my fence-building techniques. While my wife was finishing university, I had set up a natural food store in a town nearby on a major highway. To fill the shelves in summer with organic vegetables, and to fill our own freezer, I planted my own very large garden. Being poor as a church mouse, however, I couldn't afford a proper fence for it. Our landlords had a large herd of cows and some pigs, all of whom would occasionally get through the fences and head straight for the family gardens.

I had learned from fixing fences on my parents' farm that animals could sense where a fence was weak and soon, they would be through it. You could tell where the fence needed upgrading just by watching them for a while as they tested the stiffness of the fence wire and the solidness of the posts. Using that bit of knowledge, I decided to try making a fence that had all the right characteristics but without the right materials. All I could afford was a big ball of butchers' twine.

I dug in some very thick, old fence posts that I had managed to scavenge. As tightly as I could manage, I strung the twine back and forth, up and down, diagonally, tying it off in neat macramé patterns and taking it right to ground level. It had a lot more apparent substance than a regular fence, and it was a relatively pretty sight for a string fence. My neighbours and the landlord thought I was nuts, of course. So did my wife.

When the cows did eventually get out, they headed straight for the garden. The string fence design was so tightly woven that they could not even get their snouts through the gaps. And, with the string being very taut, their noses told them that the fence was very strong. Even though they could have just stepped right through the fence, snapping the string to little shreds, their noses told them that it wasn't even worth trying. I had, indeed, outsmarted the cows.

I was given to understand that something like that really impresses farmers. The kind of thing that makes them raise their Co-Op baseball caps and scratch their heads. I explained my theory was that if it looked like a strong fence and felt like a strong fence, cows would think it was a strong fence. The farmers would never have thought of trying something so obviously silly. That it worked just amazed them... and me, too! So, every summer, I wove a new impenetrable string fence around the garden.

The floors of two-hundred-year-old houses always slope to some central point where the dust bunnies handily gather. As can be expected, that was under the heavy cookstove. Our dog slept there in winter. You could see that the floor was extra-worn in that area behind the stove, not from foot traffic but from dogs and cats that had slept there for hundreds of years before ours came along. During the blizzards of winter, it was comforting to think that the pets of old would have been snug and cozy. Animals also get very affectionate when they are cooped up. That helps people and critters endure the days and nights of blowing snow.

How much snow did we get? Remember the Duclos and their neighbour across the road? One winter, there was a drift between the two peaks of their roofs across the road. You could have walked from chimney to chimney if the snow had hardened. Which it had. When the highway-sized snow-blower came up the road and disappeared into the drift, we feared the worst. However, after a minute, it emerged almost victorious on the other side of the drift. Shining brightly above the snow-blower was a nicely arched bridge of snow between the peaks of the houses. The driver even got out of the cab to have a look. If he had had a camera, I'm sure he would have wanted a picture of that one for the boys back at the works yard. Though he managed to get the drift off the road, the two houses still had an extra two metres of snow stuck to them, foundation to roof. They just left it. Good insulation and a wind break, they said.

The walls of this ancient house were at least a third of a metre thick. There were three outer layers—an original cedar shake siding, a clapboard facing, and lastly, insulbrick. The space between the inner and outer walls was filled with sawdust, old bits of cloth, hemp rope, straw, and gravel. There had been chinking in the rough-hewn boards on either side. The studs were much more robust than you find today, rough and still bearing adze marks. Most joints were fitted to cut down on the number of forged nails needed. Structural integrity came mostly from shear mass. Though strong, most old homes like this one sagged in the middle. After a few hundred years, the sag is appreciable, and nothing ever looks straight or even—not the floors, the furniture, the carpets, pictures, or tables. You learn that it is next to impossible to successfully wallpaper a room that has no square corners or level floors. We examined at least sixteen layers of paint on the kitchen wood molding and decided to add another.

Now that you know a little about this house, I can tell you how ugly it was. Grey-blue insulbrick that was a little worn and torn and buckled. A square building with two small windows on the front, separated by a door. No shutters or trim or gabling. Just everything a little cockeyed and the whole building listing slightly forward. From a distance, you would never think anyone would be living in it. Even when you got close. But we fixed it up a bit inside.

We had remarked upon the French-Canadian penchant for bright colours for their houses. English Canada is positively drab by comparison. Inside decor was a little more robust as well. We had seen burnt orange kitchens, avocado green, robin's egg blue, yellow. Our choice was purple; maybe you'd call it violet or mauve. In some lights, it was quite elegant. After twenty or thirty people said it was "interesting," we painted it pure white and stuck with that. The gleaming kitchen stuck out in sharp contrast to the surrounding environment.

Our landlords were farmers—they had pig barns, chicken barns, cow barns. It was a fragrant place. When we drove into the city, we rolled down the car windows for quite a while before we hit town. Mud and dirt dominated the landscape, except during summer, when weeds covered most of it. A small lawn lingered on in front of the house, and except for a little side garden between the house and the lane, there was nothing to pretty up the place. French Canadians then were not big on having bounteous flower gardens and shrubbery; their houses stood starkly plunked onto a plain landscape of grass. They thought that showy gardens were displays of pride. Much of the time, in English Canada, gardens merely masked some ugly houses, like ours.

One wonders how such an ugly little house could have survived for so long. Even though the landlord had grown up in the house, he was not particularly sentimental about it. He had built a nicer, new house just up the road. When we left, he wasn't sure he would rent it again or that anyone would want to rent it. He was in his sixties, and he and his wife wanted to semi-retire in town next year. His son's fiancées wanted new homes. There was an air of prosperity at that time, and everyone wanted a piece of it. Maybe the sons would use it as a granary. They weren't interested in taking over as landlords—too much work. As far as we knew, we may well have been the last people to inhabit that little abode, home for ten or more generations. On a road trip in 2017, we found it again though, all nicely modernized and pretty. It had survived yet again.

||||||||||||||||||||||||||||||||

You may remember in 1997, there was a horrific bus accident in Québec. A bus plunged over a bridge and embankment on a sharp downhill curve and forty-three passengers were killed. They were all from St. Bernard. All older folks, grandparents, aunts and uncles. A high percentage of the town's older generation was gone. These were the ones who passed on the good things, the Golden Rule, the history, the culture of the area to their children, grandchildren, and great-grandchildren. We were very saddened that those community and family voices had been suddenly silenced. No grandparents' house to visit anymore. Roots gone. The town of Saint-Bernard, Québec, created a monument to commemorate the 43 residents who died. The accident was the worst in North American history at the time. The monument serves as a place of remembrance for the community. It was such a tragedy, and I hope their families survived that awful time.

CHAPTER FOURTEEN

Longhouses, Short Memories

Mount Brydges, Ontario

There was a time, only a few generations ago on this continent, when almost everyone lived in an extended family lodging—the farmhouse. Only recently have we been reduced to living in "single family homes." Indeed, throughout most of the world, people still live in an extended family situation. Now, many people probably think that that is a bad thing, what with all the movies and books about the dastardly patriarchs or matriarchs that ruled over them. Of course, those kinds make the best movies and books—and you don't hear about all the truly good families that kept the tradition going, probably since the dawn of time as far as humans are concerned. The extended family tradition was and often still is a normal part of life for Indigenous Canadians.

After we left Québec to pursue our careers back in English Canada, we rented a rather nice country house outside a town called Mount Brydges, fifteen minutes southwest of London, Ontario. It was one of the nicer places we had had in quite a while. It was a little run down and old, but it had room—a living room a dozen people could dance wildly in without hurting each other, four bedrooms and a study, plus the usual dining room, kitchen, and bathroom. Nothing fancy, but it had nice picture windows across the front. It had all the modern conveniences, like electricity and a furnace. We hadn't had a simple thermostat to play with in over six years. However, after receiving our first oil bill, we wished we had a woodstove again.

Cookstoves or woodstoves are a lot more practical than you would think. You notice things like that when you don't have one anymore. Suddenly, we found that there was no place to go to warm your fanny or your hands. There was no place to put a large pot of water to add humidity to your house in winter. There was no place to dry out your mitts in a hurry or to warm your boots before you headed out into the snow. It got bloody cold when the hydro went out and you had no way of generating heat. A furnace is not really a convenience, just a way of producing dry heat at high cost when the hydro still works.

Once again, we were surrounded by chicken barns. Across the road were tobacco farmers with cute little square drying barns in a row. It is always informative to find that tobacco farmers are non-smokers. They are addicted to farming tobacco, however, because it is still the best-paying legal cash crop around.

The house stood where the local mill had once been. On Mill Road, naturally, the house overlooked a small dam that had once powered the mill and across the narrow road to Mill Pond. Maybe thirty metres across, the pond was fed by a wide creek at the far end. From time ago, we found a piece of the old milling stone in the embankment. We noted that the old mill ceased operating when everyone in the area switched to growing tobacco. It's too bad that farmers get paid more for growing nicotine, an addictive drug, than for growing food.

Surrounded and overhung by towering maples, willows, and alders, Mill Pond was postcard-beautiful in full fall colours. We didn't have a way of exploring the feeder creek until the next year, when we retrieved my wife's canoe from her family cottage.

On a warm fall day, Ontario's bright palate of autumn leaves carpeting the ground and floating on the water, we set out to explore the creek. Turtles lined the logs and plopped noisily into the water as we paddled by. We had heard from neighbours that the creek was a conservation area and it only went up a short way to a place where there were boardwalks and viewing towers in a marsh. Sure enough, after skimming over some very shallow areas, all overhung with pesky branches and vines, we found the source marsh and beached the canoe.

As we were pulling the canoe on shore, we were taken by surprise by a long—and I mean *long*—fence or wall, standing six metres high and made entirely of small tree trunks lashed together—with pointy tops. It was barely visible up on a higher bank and behind thick brush. As we prowled around it, we discovered that it was actually a fortified Indigenous village from the time of contact. Rebuilt and partially furnished, it was part of a settlement that had been preserved and was a local tourist attraction known as Longwoods that we knew nothing about. The neighbours didn't think to tell us that, either.

The Delaware people had a reserve only a few kilometres away, and this was a favourite pow-wow site. These people had longhouses not so long ago. Inside the walled compound, there were two main longhouses, a few other little lodges, a bear pit, a root cellar, and not much else. They lived in family groupings in the longhouses, maybe four, five, or six families in smaller longhouses and ten or more in big ones. There were no dividing walls, no doors. Maybe skins separated some areas.

You may wonder about the bear pit. Not many houses have one these days. I had to ask about that. The pit was about two metres deep and covered like a flattened teepee with large poles. Evidently, the bear, possibly a young one, was trapped somehow and then taken to the village and caged there until fresh meat was needed in the winter. Cattle are a little less trouble, I would guess.

You may also remember that, as a child, I marvelled at the people who had brought down a woolly mammoth twelve thousand years ago, in a field only a half-day's walk away. Perhaps these villagers were their direct descendants. Perhaps bears were not so fearsome compared to woolly mammoths.

It is interesting to think about group house living. We see the world differently depending on our housing. What becomes of privacy when you live openly with a dozen or more others under one roof—and *in the same room*? Does it matter that everyone would know whose kid was bed-wetting, who was having nooky, and who farted? Probably not. They also got to see the love and attention that families heaped on each other living this close. Just a really big family by current standards. A very close family.

The walled fortification around the village was also a maze. All around, there were two walls of pointed wood staves, with a two-metre corridor between them. Along the top of the innermost wall, on the inside, was a walkway from which to shoot arrows or throw spears down at marauding, unwelcome visitors. The entrances to the village had three sets of walls, with dead-end passages leading off two of the three—again to trap marauders. The dead-ends could be changed from year to year, letting this year's well-worn path in lead to a dead-end. Modern "gated" communities could learn a thing or two here.

I revisited Longwoods thirty years ago with our young son. This time I thought about it in new ways. During my final year at university in 1970, I had done my big paper on the impact that Western religions had had on reserves in Ontario. One of the reserves I visited as part of my research was the Six Nations Reserve near Brantford, about one hundred kilometres to the east. I had some trouble at the time getting to talk to members of the Longhouse religion, the remnants of the religious beliefs and practices of these Native peoples.

I remember many people, white and Indigenous, saying that the Indigenous people still holding onto the Longhouse religious beliefs were trouble. First, they weren't Christian, and second, they still believed in the hereditary chief system of government. Hereditary Native governance systems (both patriarchal and matriarchal) were banned long ago by the Canadian federal government, and in their place the government ordered elected band councils. There continues to be trouble to this day about this issue on many reserves across Canada. It was much easier for outsiders and governments to manipulate elected councils. You can influence who gets elected much easier than you can bloodlines – those born into power through their family. We would call that royalty, but they did not think of Chieftainship that way. One had a responsibility for the tribe, and it was not for personal enrichment.

Since I first learned about the hereditary system, I have spent much time actively engaged in electoral politics at all levels of government, from the community to the national level. I now have a great deal more respect for the hereditary form of government.

Imagine, if you will for a minute, that you have been born as the next chief of your clan or village. You grow up knowing that. You know everyone in your group, their capacities and shortcomings, your history and your present circumstances. One day, you will be responsible for the wellbeing of all your people. You are prepared for that role every day of your younger life. It is both an honour and a burden bestowed upon you, and there is nothing you can do to avoid it short of dying or running away. Let's take for granted that you do take your role seriously, and you do your utmost as chief to care for and lead your people, thinking ahead seven generations, as is the custom.

Compare that to the seriousness and knowledge of many of your short-term elected politicians today. By whom would you feel most comfortable being governed?

You see the dilemma? Democracy does have its shortcomings.

||||||||||||||||||||||||||||||||

We spent four happy years in the Mill Pond house. The rent was remarkably cheap, and we had a good-sized vegetable garden.

Almost all the houses we have lived in for the past twenty-eight years have had room for a vegetable garden. Few of them started out with one, but turning sod and putting one in is the first thing we did when we arrived. All summer long and into the fall and winter, most of what appears on our dinner plates (except the meat and fish) comes from our garden—and from fruit trees if we have been lucky enough to have those, too. If you have only eaten from supermarket bins, you don't know what fresh produce really tastes like.

Having an over-abundance of produce also gives you gifts or something to barter with, and a handy excuse to visit your neighbours. A bag of potatoes for a dozen eggs. A basket of apples for a basket of tomatoes. Mason jars of beets, antipasto, chutney, or homemade ketchup for last winter's plowing of your drive. You can't imagine what homemade fresh ketchup tastes like. I can't either right now, since I've had trouble growing enough tomatoes in the rainy climate I now live in! Our neighbours at the Mill Pond house made the very best ketchup.

I notice now, almost fifty years later, that many people still have vegetable gardens in their backyards, but few people have tended to the fruit trees that were planted there decades ago. The fruit trees are tall and unpruned, and bear poorly. Such a shame that we are losing these skills or have no time to tend to our trees. Fruit helps us meet our neighbours and build community. Being part of a community where people care for each other is probably the most important thing you do need.

CHAPTER FIFTEEN

Prairie Houses

Leaving Ontario to live in Vancouver was a decision we took after driving across Canada three summers in a row. Enthralled by the West Coast, we camped our way from north to south, even hiking the Chilkoot gold rush trail in the Yukon and paddling down the Yukon River. We didn't really want to go back to Ontario after the mountains and ocean had seeped into our being. And so we moved out west.

We noticed a few differences about the West and its housing—there was nothing very old, like in Québec or even Ontario, and the designs were more basic than pretty. Stone or brick houses are few and far between. History is shorter. There is often a fly-by-night goldrush tackiness to northern towns. Earlier prairie homes, like sod houses and log cabins, could still be seen off the main highways.

Age is a relative thing in some parts, though. On one of our continent crossings, we decided on the northern route (we never drove the same roads twice if we could avoid it) and planned to look up a few old friends who lived along the way. One of these was Claire, who we had met in Québec City five years before. We heard that she had returned to her home in Saskatchewan to take up farming on her family's homestead. This was a challenging thing for a young woman to do, and so we decided to pay her a visit.

Those of you who have driven across the prairies for the first time will remember the awe of unending flatness for hours on end. We had only seen the southern parts before, and from the road, at least, the north didn't look any different. The only let-up in the flat relief would be valleys cut down into the prairie. This surprised us at first. All of a sudden from out of nowhere, the road dipped down into a lush river valley with trees and a higher, more interesting horizon than the one we had just disappeared under. And then up you would go, back to the featureless horizon.

To be honest, the prairies are not featureless but repetitious. For a while, you see huge square chunks of brilliant yellow where canola or mustard grows. Then come the greens of lentils or rye, the golden browns of wheat and barley, or in spring and fall, the very dark brown of freshly turned fields. Farmhouses, barns, silos and farm machinery appear from time to time. Hydro poles and towers run on out of sight, straight and perfect.

Most of the newer farmhouses were huge versions of suburban ranchers, looking out of place on the prairie. The older homes were converted into granaries or, occasionally, into drive sheds. The really old ones, the ones built of chinked logs with sod roofs, stood forsaken and overgrown with weeds. Wistful memories. Gravestones.

We found Vaun on the map just below Jackfish Lake and drove on into the town. Like hundreds of others just like it, Vaun was a small town, frozen in time some thirty years prior. Nothing was new, many houses were run down, and some were empty. The typical dying prairie town.

We only had a general delivery address to go on, so we stopped at the post office/general store/gas station/billiard room/hotel in the centre of the town of maybe fifteen houses. There being only enough business in town for one store, it had a little bit of everything you could imagine. Jeans, boots, biscuits, mayonnaise, stove oil, nails, pipe, billiards, a few rooms for rent… The owner was behind the counter, thankfully, and we asked our question.

"Sure. She lives in the new house at the top of the hill," he told us matter-of-factly.

He even took us outside and pointed the direction and repeated, "The new house at the top of the hill there." And then he disappeared back into the store. Did he actually point at the house, or just in that direction? We didn't know.

My wife and I looked in that direction and back to each other several times. At first, all we could see was a flat road heading out of town and a half-dozen old houses. There was nothing approaching a *new* house in sight. Maybe there was a hill far off in the distance, but I couldn't see it. I did bend down, sort of at car-bumper height, to see if I could make out any features on the horizon. It was then that I noticed there was indeed a very slight rise going up the road. Maybe enough of a rise that at the top, if you turned a hose on, the water would generally run down it toward town instead of just puddling in one spot, as it usually did.

I pointed this out to my wife, who also bent down for a look. She began looking at the houses more carefully now. Yes, they were all old, but some were older than others. Most were the typical square, two-storey clapboard box, but one was definitely an early rancher style. If you considered time a relative thing, it was a new house. Could it be …?

Rather than risk the embarrassment of going back into the store to accuse the owner of shucking us when he might not be, we decided to head up to the "new" house at the top of the hill. Claire greeted us at the door in stunned amazement.

"How did you find me all the way out here?!"

She laughed and laughed. So did we.

"It was easy," we said. "We got directions at the store down the hill."

Claire was indeed farming the land. We watched as she climbed onto her tractor to park it and some machinery out of the way so we could drive in behind the house and park our car. She looked to be every bit as much a part of her large, dusty tractor as any man would. Prairie dust does not discriminate.

We learned that she and her older sister had seeded about a section with five different crops between themselves. We were told the things farmers must think about while they are on their tractors. Which crops would bring in good money. Which crops might not, because everybody was growing them and would flood the market. Worrying about rail strikes or port worker strikes or wheat sales to China. There was so much to think about when riding a tractor out here.

Things were going well for Claire, but she was mostly there because of her aging father. She and her sister had agreed that they would live with their dad until he died. The sister had returned from the romance of fishing in Ketchekan, Alaska. Claire, we knew from Québec, but also from the Yukon, where she had recently ventured, met a nice fellow, and lived half the year. We saw their gorgeous log house and log sauna by a river, but they weren't home when we visited that particular summer.

On Claire's farm, the old family homestead still stood, somewhere between recovery and demolition, off in another field. Prairie folk never seem to tear buildings down. They just let them slowly wobble, bend, twist, and sink into the ground. It's as if tearing them down would be too decisive, too final. Or maybe they leave them up just to relieve the boredom of the endless horizon. Eventually, I guess, as they slowly rot into the stubble fields, they could make small hills that you could build another house on top of. You could see *more* of the endless horizon.

Claire took us to the homestead on a hot and dusty prairie afternoon. I have seen many of these old, grey houses staring vacant eyed on vast stretches of field. Kind of like a house-sized human skull, the eye sockets are the two tall, black windows on either side of a single darkened doorway, the mouth full open and frozen. It sits darkly and forebodingly on the land, as if it has lost something vital that may or may not come back. Dead, it seems to wait, nonetheless.

A few times, Claire and her sister talked about and then put aside the idea of making the place livable again. There were fine trees and berry patches around the house. It was not out in a field but nestled among poplar and aspen trees that rustled so loudly in the constant breeze that you could not hear a person talking across the yard. This kind of coziness was a little odd on the prairies, where most preferred the endless vistas and seamless sky.

In the end, the pioneering spirit that they inherited from this prairie homestead also took the sisters away. They were strong and resourceful, and did men's work and women's work, and traveled to far off places both culturally and geographically. I haven't heard from Claire since. I'm sure the sisters kept the farm when their dad died. I can see them going back every once in a while to plant a crop themselves rather just leasing the land out all the time. But they also have other lives and other places to be. They have both roots and webs.

CHAPTER SIXTEEN

Maritime Wilderness

Brighton Beach, North Vancouver, British Columbia

Maybe it was the mountain air. Or the vistas. Or the vast wilderness areas. Or the ocean. Or all the above. After spending three summer holidays in a row in British Columbia, it became increasingly difficult to drive back to smug and smoggy Ontario. My wife and I were attracted to BC because of the easy access to these wonderful wilderness spaces. Beyond that, it was enough of a lure that we would leave all our relatives five thousand kilometres behind us.

We needed a city, however, in which to find work.

Wilderness and major cities come together, not always amicably, in many parts of Western Canada. Bears and cougars regularly drop into the suburbs that abut the wilderness and mountains on the northern edge of metropolitan Vancouver—North and West Vancouver. We quickly determined that we couldn't afford to live there. Only expensive houses have the luxury of dangerous wildlife roaming their backyards.

On arriving in the Vancouver area, we rented a basement suite in the distant suburb of Surrey at an outrageous rental rate. It was a shock to us to be paying big-city prices in a hot housing market like nothing we had ever experienced before. Fortunately, there was bush out the back of this house.

On the other side, we discovered the local nudist colony. BC has all kinds of wildlife. We quickly set about trying to find something that was a little rural, maybe, and hopefully much cheaper than anything we had seen so far.

On one of our forays, we had driven out to the end of the road at Belcarra Park, which lies on the east side of Indian Arm, a saltwater inlet that stretches up twenty kilometres north of Vancouver. Sheer mountainsides on both shores slide down to the water, and no roads beyond this point. The access road seemed a long way out of Vancouver, and so we thought the housing prices there would be cheaper. A vacant cliffside waterfront lot was going for three hundred thousand dollars. Houses rented for fifteen hundred. This was a chic area to live in. We had also brought our new canoe along and so decided to enjoy the day touring up Indian Arm, even though we couldn't afford to buy any of its beachfront rocks.

To cover some distance, I snapped on a yammering two-horse motor, and we set out. After a few bays of lovely glass-and-wood West Coast mansions on the water, the last road ended, and we entered two hours of wilderness. Occasionally there would be a little dock sticking out and a cabin or two tucked up on a little bit of flat space. Summer places. Fish camps. One, far up the arm, had a "For Sale" sign on it that quoted a price of thirty-five thousand dollars. Now, that was more like it!

At the head of the arm was the Wigwam Inn. It looked nothing like a wigwam, but Canadians like those kinds of names. It had the right cachet for a place at the mouth of the Indian River. It had several lives, as a swank club in the twenties, a gaming and whoring house to loggers in the thirties and forties, nothing in the fifties, a haven for hippies in the sixties. It was again being brought back to swank status in the early 1980s. We arrived in our canoe, very much out of place, with the yachts moored at the dock. Feeling a tad shabby and smelling a little of gas, we struck up conversations with the staff rather than the clientele.

One jovial and matter-of-fact little woman with a British accent told us that there were several places for sale on the Arm, and there might be places for rent, too. She told us about the place where she lived down Indian Arm and told us to go visit there. She chirped, "I live there year-round and go everywhere by boat. So do lots of people up this way." This was news to us, so we followed her directions.

Brighton Beach was the name of the little community we came to. A dozen or so cabins were arranged higgledy-piggledy across a cliff face and up a triangular field of grass. There were a few nice-looking cabins and a few mouldering ones tipping into the ground. We later learned that the community originated just after the war. From the auspices of a local legion, the land was purchased as a cooperative, and only veterans could buy into it for a paltry fee. Once admitted, you were then given a "lot" on which to build your cabin.

It had been a summer place in the beginning, but a few people were now living there year-round. There were five or six older couples with grown or teenage kids that came up for most of the summer. Patrick, a wildlife officer, lived in one cabin near the water, and a family of four lived just above. Above them were two younger women. Out on the cliffside were three places, one the cabin belonging to the lady we met at the inn and her disabled husband, another a flashy place with lots of deck owned by a pile-driver fellow, and a party place, perched the highest and furthest out.

After touring the area with one of the residents who greeted us at the dock, we had one phone number to call about one of the older log cabins high up in the back of the field. We also had a lot of thinking to do. There was no road, no hydro, and the on-the-ground PVC pipe water distribution system didn't look promising. When we returned home, we called the number and found out that the place was not for rent after all. And that was the end of that.

I was working in student services at the British Columbia Institute of Technology at that time, and Monday morning was our departmental meeting—the table was made up of many people - me - student affairs (my job), student health, financial aid, the registrar, student housing, and the counselling division. After the meeting, we all went for coffee break. Responding to the "What did you do this weekend?" question, I told them about our canoeing up Indian Arm looking for a place to rent. I noticed that many people began smiling, especially the head of student counselling. "Go on. Go on," they said. So, I finished my story.

Well, surprise, surprise! The head of counselling owned one of the cabins at Brighton Beach, and many of the people around the table had been up there for barbecue parties. And it might be that his cabin was available for rent. Later, he told us his marriage had broken up and the teenage kids were not at all interested in going up there anymore—and neither were he and his ex-wife. So, yes, we could rent it if we really wanted to. Did we know what we were getting into? Of course not.

He took us up to Brighton in his runabout the next weekend. We had missed seeing the cabin he owned on our first trip. The reason was salmon berries. For those of you who don't know salmon berries, they are a lot like blackberries or raspberries except the fruit is orange, yellow, or sometimes red, and not too sweet, rather juicy and a little fuzzy on the outside and seedy on the inside. And they grow to be three metres tall or more. They can hide a cabin.

After chain-sawing a path to the cabin, we were pleasantly surprised to see a fairly new, one-and-a-half-storey A-frame cabin with large picture windows and a lovely sun deck. The cabin was the farthest back and highest up—the view was spectacular. We were hooked. And the price was right: $150 a month, about a fifth of what we were paying for a crummy basement suite.

Mind you, we had to buy a boat, pay for moorage at a marina, run the boat back and forth daily, and buy propane for the stove and hot water heater. Still, that only worked out to about half of what we were currently paying. So, the big decision was whether we could handle the lifestyle—what it would take to live in that little cabin with the million-dollar view. It's a little like *The Beachcombers* TV show, where you are out in boats all day and surrounded by wilderness. For those of you who watched the CBC show *Danger Bay*, this was the precise locale. Real danger never materialized, though—except in weather form.

We knew how to rough it after having had similar household inconveniences in Boulter, Ontario and St. Bernard, Québec. The big difference here was commuting by boat every day to the marina, where the car was parked, and then carrying on to work. The run was about seven nautical miles, down a wide channel, through some little islands and rocks, around a bend, past a few oil refineries, and into the marina. Watching out for the giant freighters anchored here and there or being towed in one direction or another! They don't get out of your way.

My wife, Kate, had spent much of her youth in canoes and her family boat. I had done the same, but had spent more time with power boats, water-skiing and fishing and duck hunting and just bombing around. By the time I was sixteen, I was seasoned enough to run safely in very rough weather on Lake Nippissing, Ontario, where my family lived on the water for four years, if you remember. I felt comfortable about the boating, though I hadn't been in a power boat in fifteen years.

So, we bought a decent boat, five and half metres long with a good size inboard/outboard motor and a full camper top—and a chainsaw. The boat fit somewhere in between the little runabouts with outboards and the small cabin cruisers moored at Brighton Beach's wharf. We hoped it would do. The chainsaw kept the salmon berries at bay and cut our winter wood.

When it came time to move there, it rained steadily, as it had for the past sixty days. It was early May, but you wouldn't know it. Depressing to those of us used to a little more sun in our lives. The move took eight boat trips and forty-four wheelbarrow loads. Sofas, beds, you name it, it all went from a truck at the marina, out on tippy docks and little fingers and into the boat, up to Brighton, out onto more tippy fingers, up the ramp and into a wheelbarrow for the rest of the trip about 170 metres up a steady incline to our lovely cabin with the great view. *Pheeeeewww.*

Our first initiation to the fraternity of Brighton Beach came with the annual clean-out of the reservoir. Water for the cabins came from a dammed-up creek that flowed through the property. The dam was simple—a few wide planks, a sluice gate, lots of big boulders and sheets of plastic. The men had long ago dug out a fair-sized pond to hold the water for the community's use. Problem was, Mother Nature filled it up with debris and silt every winter. But all we had to do was remove it every spring.

Six men, hip-deep in muck, surrounded by six more, knee-deep in it, kept up a steady stream of mud from shovel to bucket to the guy on shore, who tossed it downstream and into the forest. Messy work - mud, mud, mud coated us all, coated the tree trunks, rocks, and forest floor all around us. We had created a filthy eyesore that would again be our water supply when it cleared. It was heavy work, but we lived up to the Brighton Beach motto I learned that day: "We may be slow, but we're sloppy." After a few quick fills and drains of the pond, the last of the mud washed away and the pond filled up quite clear. I can't say that we or the forest looked any better.

Similar work parties attacked the wharf for annual repairs and tended the lawn and shrubs. With similar results. They all worked fine afterwards and looked a mess. The grass was always too long before it was cut and never raked up. The wharf, floats, and fingers came apart several times a year.

It was at these work parties that we got to know the community dynamics. There were two camps. One was the year-rounders, who thought the "summer sunshine" folk were wussies compared to those who stuck it out all year. And then there were the wussies. Most of them wanted to have a road built into the place, pushing the value of the land up into the millions and making everybody rich. Or so the story went. The permanent residents liked their isolation, the rugged back-to-nature thing and the cheap living.

Many of the old-timers were now into their sixties, and only one older couple stayed all year—Andy and Molly. They had built a cozy and functional cabin on a cliffside looking down the Arm into Vancouver. Hanging on only by its pillars and posts cemented into the rock face, the cabin was accessed via a treacherous cliff path or via its own floating dock bolted to the cliff. On the second landing up from the dock was a hot tub facing south, and nothing between it and Vancouver—or the City of Burnaby, technically. The cabin on the next level up was rustic but well done. Andy was an electrician. Molly took care of the place. They hunted and fished and camped on their holidays up in Cariboo country—getting away from it all, you know.

Andy had one of those boats they call a skiff, with a stand-up wheelhouse on it. It was a flat-bottomed, flat-sided, flat-fronted aluminum box with an outboard motor hanging off the back. The wheelhouse looked like a telephone booth with a slightly sloped front window. It did not have any creature comforts, but you could get it dirty and leave it that way, and nobody would notice. Andy liked that feature in a boat. His wood supply came from what he fished out of the salt chuck. Andy had it all figured out and lived the life as successfully as anyone could.

The first gorgeous summer passed, and we began to dig in for the coming winter, whatever that would be. Some people said it could be cold and snowy, and some said probably just rainstorms this year. They didn't know. We didn't know. West Coast weather is like that. West Coast people talk about the weather like that.

We replaced a puny open fireplace with a Baby Bear woodstove, insulated under the cabin, and put on weather stripping and plastic over the non-view windows. That seemed about all we could do for this little cabin of forty square metres with a vaulted roof and walls that had no insulation. Single-pane windows, too. More wood needed.

Getting your wood supply on a mountain slope heading into the ocean is not easy. First off, the terrain is really an oversized obstacle course of huge fallen trees, stumps, desk-size boulders, brambles, and creeks. There is enough standing dead wood that you don't have to venture too far to find it. The first rule is to look only uphill from your cabin. That way, you carry it down.

Without the benefit of even a path that a wheelbarrow could follow, I devised a stretcher with extra-long handles to cart the wood back to the cabin. It was relatively easy to manage a large load, even hopping stepping stones across creeks. Others borrowed it, a sign of something truly useful. The hardest part of the work was getting the wood ready for carting. Many tree trunks were more than a metre across and had to be split up before the chunks would fit securely on the stretcher. Mature trees back east were like mere kindling here. But at least the eastern trees were mostly hardwood and burned a lot longer than the pine and fir trees here. Felling, bucking, splitting, carting. *It's free*, we kept telling ourselves. Only a few visits to the chiropractor to account for.

Frozen water lines, a foot of snow, and our boat frozen in place in a sheet of ice surrounding the dock told us winter had indeed arrived one morning. Now, you wouldn't think anyone would be stupid enough to go boating in that kind of weather, would you? There were all kinds of boats merrily heading down the Arm on their regular commute. Even the younger people at Brighton were down at the dock sweeping the snow off their boats, chipping ice off the ropes and rocking the floats. The waves from the floats broke up the sheet of ice. And the water taxi came in to pick up a few children for their daily ride to school.

The locals told us stories about people driving full tilt into a sheet of ice and neatly slicing the bottoms of their boats off. "Maybe *their* bottoms, too," they said.

If you go slowly, a good fibreglass boat can crunch through a few centimetres or more of ice. Thicker than that and you have to break it up by doing power donuts to send a large wake into the ice sheet. It works, and you proceed another twenty or thirty boat-lengths or so. We had to do this many times over the course of two winters where our freshwater stream emptied into the Arm. Freshwater floats on top of saltwater.

I must tell you that while we were working on such problems, the surrounding snow-covered mountains and black ocean water on a sunny winter's day were absolutely breathtaking. How it could be so cold, so snowy, and yet still have open water in Indian Arm (mostly) for boating was unusual to us Easterners.

Our first winter break, we had traveled to Ontario for Christmas and returned the day before New Year's Eve. We saw that Vancouver had just been hit by another deep cold and snowy spell, and we had to struggle to get from the airport to the marina. Trudging through a foot of snow and surveying the ice sheet and our snowbound boat, we stopped and laughed. And took a picture of the scene—it was dark, but the snow and a clear night gave a gentle glow to everything.

We made our way up the arm under the starriest sky we had seen. There were very few lights on up our way, and we realized that the hydro was out. The few lights were kerosene or gas lamps. Mostly, though, it seemed like nobody was home up our way. We couldn't even see Brighton Beach, because not one light shone. First time we'd ever seen that. There were no boats at the dock. It was spooky!

Indeed, we were utterly alone. Just us in the freezing cold in the middle of nowhere, trying to get the woodstove going to thaw out the cabin and ourselves. Not even the younger people or the old-time locals had stayed through this. We were Eastern wussies no more. Our ace was that cold and snow was something we could cope with just fine.

Fog, now that was another thing altogether. You live on the ocean, you get fog. We had mastered all that the ocean could throw at us—which was quite a bit—monstrous seas, sheets of rain, darkness and snowstorms that had no finish on the water. The snow simply disappeared into the water. You get surrounded and mesmerized by zillions of snowflakes, and then they hit the water and are gone. The water is unmoved, untouched, unaffected. But fog just *is*. Is everywhere.

We tried coping with the fog in several ways. This meant doing a slow run from the marina in Port Moody to Brighton, and the other way, too. While doing this, we carefully noted our compass bearings, the rpm of the motor, and the time we ran in one direction before turning around points, rocks, islands, and so on to our destination. We tried to factor in the tides, too.

For the most part, the system worked well, until one winter when we installed a window defroster fan. The first foggy morning, we set out on our compass bearings, with the defroster doing a wonderful job. First, there was a sixteen-minute straight run on open water. As usual, there was absolutely nothing to see. You could make out things maybe five or ten metres ahead of the bow. Keeping your eyes focused on nothing is very tiring and quirky because you can imagine seeing things that aren't there. When there is nothing to see, you have no perspective or background to work with. What did come into view this morning was a dock, only ten minutes into the trip.

We had never seen this dock before, and on motoring slowly a bit farther, we came to the end of a bay we had not seen before. How could this be? Ten slow minutes from home? Maybe it was the Twilight Zone, we thought. A parallel universe.

Finally, my wife recognized something—and though I disputed it, she was right in the end. We had crossed Indian Arm instead of going down it, because the fan motor had pulled the compass off course exactly twenty-five degrees. Somehow, we never saw the rocky point and all the rocks and islands at the mouth of the bay we had come to the end of. It took some doing to work our way out of it.

This was only the beginning of the adventure. We had no compass bearings to get us from here to where we wanted to go—or back home for that matter—so we crept along, hugging the shoreline. There was one point where we had to cross a nautical mile of open water and get to the other side to find the marina. This area was where the huge freighters anchored. We turned off our motor at one point to see if we could hear them. Nope. Dead quiet. No. Maybe a foghorn or two in the distance. It was hard to say exactly which direction and how far.

Kate had the job of using our foghorn—a tin-can-sized air horn. When you motor in the fog, you have to sound a horn or bell to let others know where you are. Or at least that you are out there, *somewhere*. The first thing Kate learned about the foghorn was to open up the boat top and point the horn outside before squeezing the trigger. The other things she was supposed to have learned were the horn signals for telling another boat whether you are moving or stationary and which side you are passing them on. We heard other horns, but not too close by. When the side of a freighter loomed up not six metres in front of us out of the fog, we nearly jumped out of our skins.

The horn signals Kate emitted at that precise moment told the ship's crew that we were circling it in zigzag fashion, I think. Four or five smiling crewmen appeared about ten metres up and hung over the railing to see what the commotion was about. Kate of course noticed this, too. She huffed and gave them a blast as we headed into the fog once again. It was then that we heard the ship's foghorn. When you are in a little wee boat and close to a freighter, its foghorn is some twenty metres up and over the deck. It could be a long way away for all you can tell in the sound shadow of the ship.

When you hear an echo of your own horn, you are about to see the side of another freighter close up—was the next thing we abruptly learned. And so, we made it to the marina. Miraculously, we still weren't late for work (never were), even though the road traffic was just creeping along, too.

By the time the second winter came, we had gained both hydro and a phone, making us feel downright civilized. We had also gained the friendship of many of the permanent residents and began to socialize much more.

Perhaps the most memorable night we had at Brighton was Christmas evening over at Andy and Molly's place which hung off the cliff. This was our first Christmas in British Columbia, and we were feeling a little better about it because it was starting to snow. On the coast, you are more apt to have a green Christmas. Landlubbers that we were, we had no idea how one celebrated Christmas when living on the water.

At about eight o'clock, the partygoers were told to go out to the hot tub on the lower deck. We were looking forward to this, even with the snow! So, there we are in the hot tub, which is bolted to the cliff-face, and looking down Indian Arm toward Vancouver, maybe eleven kilometres away. Except this night, you could hardly see the wharf because of the snow. The wind was up a little, but relaxing in the hot tub was more than bearable. Then we heard music coming from out in the snowstorm, out on the water—blaring carol music.

Dimly at first, twinkly coloured lights swayed back and forth in the whiteness of the snow—rows of them, strings of them—bobbing and brightening. Out of the snowstorm and black water below came a flotilla of some twenty boats all bedecked with Christmas lights running along the gunwales, up the guy wires, and around their decks. Each vessel had its own design and colour scheme and some had their own loudspeakers echoing recorded Christmas music and carols off our cliff.

The lead boat, twenty metres long, maybe, made a close pass of the dock so the captain could come on deck and wish us partygoers all a Merry Christmas—each of us by name—and a ho-ho-ho from our neighbours at the local marina. Making a large circle right in front of us, the boats paraded once around and then headed off into the snow again. Soon their caroling sounds were swallowed up by the snow and wind and we were just sitting there in this hot tub on a cliff in a snowstorm.

Later, we found out that there are more elaborate and orchestrated carol ship tours and parties organized all around Vancouver near Christmas. This local marina effort was far beyond our imagining, but not an isolated event. For those of you who have not experienced the carol ships, let me just say that there is something very eerily beautiful in the carrying of sound across water and in the twinkly reflections of Christmas lights on the water. It is a unique and joyous combination of gorgeous sights and sounds. I'm not sure how far this tradition extends in maritime Canada, but it is a damn fine tradition to have!

The cabin at Brighton Beach began losing its allure by the third year. A teenage son of one of the crankier owners built a cabin right next to ours, in the little glen of trees where the deer used to come in the morning and came no more. Even the bears stopped coming onto the deck to neatly eat all the nasturtium flowers in our long planter boxes. And then they'd poop on the deck. Most of the fuchsia bushes were gone, and so too the noisy swarms of hummingbirds that had eaten there. I should say that hummers really like the colour red. They poke their little beaks and tongues into anything red. Quite fearless and rather curious, hummers forced Kate to give up wearing her red two-piece bathing suit. *Bzzzzt*. Poke. Poke. *Bzzzt*. Poke. Poke.

My wife, Kate, is a teacher, and she had a Grade 5 class at this time, and they were always interested to hear about her Brighton adventures. Almost daily, something unusual or interesting would occur. Patrick, our neighbour, was a wildlife conservation officer who was as rugged and wily as they come. Handsome and adventurous, his best friend was his dog, a border collie type. Their adventures always kept the kids glued to their seats. Patrick mostly kayaked back and forth from Deep Cove, with the dog up front in the luggage bay. One time, on a snowy, blowy night, the dog tipped the kayak, barking at a cormorant that had suddenly surfaced. They had to swim to shore with the kayak in tow, empty it, get in again, and continue on. Patrick was so mad. Got his groceries all wet. Stupid dog. Normal people would have died instantly. Patrick was just annoyed for a day.

Then there was the day when the dog got trapped in a debris torrent of logs rushing down a river (which Patrick was investigating). The last Patrick saw of his dog was it clinging desperately to a log as it disappeared down rapids and around the bend. A two-hour search of the shoreline turned up no sign of the dog. On the drive out, some ten kilometres on, the dog was waiting patiently by the side of the road, quite glad to see Patrick. Again, Patrick was just annoyed for a day.

Patrick's dog did not take kindly to the skunks living under one of the cabins. Then, Patrick was just annoyed for several days. After a couple of years Patrick took off for Florida to help on an endangered species ranch. We heard he had come back the next year and headed north to log with horses, something which he had done before. Haven't heard from him since.

We also had stories about our other neighbours and the wildlife regulars we knew along the way. We cruised with a killer whale one morning, watched a seal struggle for hours with a large fish wedged the wrong way in its throat, knew where the flashy harlequin ducks hung out, counted the herons in the heronry—a huge but dead tree. Up to fifteen would be up there, perching as far from each other as possible. Not very sociable types.

We loved our neighbourhood, but the lifestyle and the local social environment was getting tougher. It was time to move on.

We had saved enough money, and the housing market had crashed in the meantime, so we bought a townhouse near the marina and became summer sun-shiners at Brighton for a few more summers, and then finally gave it up. It had been life in wilderness, on ocean, in nature, on adventure and wonderment.

The cabin did well when we left. Its new owners, two women who owned an older place just down the hill bought it, carpeted it, fixed up the kitchen and bathroom, and added a deck and hot tub out the back. It's not the same place at all now, but it still takes the same breed of people to live there. A cabin in the bush is an experience worth having. Don't mind the bears—but I hope you find good neighbours.

CHAPTER SEVENTEEN

Townhomes and Community

East Hill Townhouse, Port Moody, British Columbia

Discovering that the only housing we could afford to buy (with a hefty mortgage) would be a townhouse, we lowered our expectations. Townhouses, for those of you who may be unfamiliar with them, are kind of like row houses, only more expensive and with huge carports or garage doors for fronts. A row house usually has a back lane for parking. The front is devoted to porches and a bit of lawn or garden boxes and a sidewalk. A townhouse complex looks more like it was designed for cars, not people. I think the architect for our complex knew how ugly the street and carports would be. There was only one window facing the street, the kitchen window, and all the rest were on the back, green belt side.

If it is an owner-based townhouse complex, a strata corporation, the rules for colour conformity and tidiness are usually prevalent. Spiff and emptiness is what you see. In rental townhouses, you see the neatnik and the pack rat, the eccentric and the extrovert and boats and tent trailers parked. Ours was of the owner variety, and a rather large complex—144 units.

Apart from the brutal asphalt and carport syndrome, the townhouse complex we moved into had some positive features, too. Between the streets of natural cedar-sided townhouses ran a green belt with tall evergreens and new play areas and sandboxes for kids. On the east and south sides, the complex was bounded by tall trees, a steep gully, and a stream. On the north was a forest that later came down to make way for a new subdivision. Looking up, you could almost imagine yourself in a forest. Looking down, however, you couldn't avoid seeing the cars. We also had a pool, right at the stop sign where cars turned or came past on both sides. Always surrounded by cars.

Everyone needed cars, including us. The complex was not near anything. You drove to school, to shop, to work, to the library, to the recreation centre. It's too bad that planners can't seem to create enough complexes and houses side by side to then build in all those amenities within walking distance. Air pollution is a problem here, and we were part of the problem.

Living cheek by jowl with other people was something we had almost forgotten. The farmhouses and the cabin were more to our liking than the noisy and lively townhouse complex. You couldn't avoid your neighbours and got to know many of them more than you would have liked. You did meet good people, too. Fortunately, living in a strata because you can have rules and limits to noise or messes, you get to deal with those who are really bothersome, but there weren't many of those here. Sometimes, however, you realize that you are one of the bothersome ones.

Adjusting to the rules and to close living is a bit of challenge to those of us used to wide open spaces. I sold my electric guitar and amplifier. What's the use in having one if you can't crank it up or have even noisier friends over for a jam session? And, thinking positively, you can then again appreciate the acoustic guitar sound, even if you can't sing very loudly.

Younger people seemed to have louder car stereo systems than they had in their townhouses. I sold my chainsaw. Nothing to cut anymore. We decided not to keep our boat—because year-round moorage cost too much and we couldn't store the boat on a trailer at our townhouse. And you couldn't tear motors apart and leave them strewn about your carport while you waited for parts or time to put them back together again. You could leave your car and a rake or broom or bicycle there and that was all. Neatness has a certain visual appeal, but you can't do much with it.

Our son was born here. A townhouse is a good place for those with young families. There is no shortage of new parents who can identify with you and help you out when you need it. In previous generations, we had a large extended family close by to help us young parents. Our families lived three thousand kilometres away—or rather, we did. Now it is our neighbours who help. The neighbourhood family.

A few hours after arriving home from the hospital, babe in arms, we started getting advice from near strangers on things that we had never heard of, like breast pumps. You have no idea what will come out of people's mouths when you tell them about your troubles with babies. Why don't schools prepare you for the real things in life? Like breast pumps. We didn't even hear about those in pre-natal classes.

A quick word on pre-natal classes. Why on Earth they don't tell you about what happens when you get home with the baby is a mystery. That's when you really need to know stuff. We used a midwife for the labour and birth (in the hospital, where it was encouraged by our doctor), and that's all you need for the pre-natal part. How to cope once you get home is what you really need to know, and nobody prepared us for that. Thanks to our neighbours with young children, we learned about breast pumps, about how to get a diaper tight enough so that it didn't leak, about slings and rocking chairs and all the other important stuff that can make your life as baby parents more livable.

The baby stage lasts such a short time, even though it seems much longer when it is your first. Our little guy was up walking a week before he was nine months old. A great feat, I know, but try keeping track of someone that young and small who can disappear in an instant. Soon after mastering flat surfaces, he wanted outside to try real terrain. Speed bumps were a hit. Up and down. Gravel is trouble to walk on but tastes great. Sand, too. A townhouse complex is a relatively safe place to have toddlers if you don't mind what they eat.

Children can play safely on the streets that become quiet after 9 a.m. There are hordes of other children to play with. You always hear the sounds of children playing outside, except on rainy days, when you hear them bouncing off the walls next door. Daycare or babysitting is readily available. And everyone knows daycare moms and what they are like. Some left the TV on and filled their places with toys, while others organized daily outings and crafts and played with the children. Each to their own style. Both kinds were always busy.

We found plenty of people trying to make the best of our complex. These good folk were busy organizing Christmas parties for the kids and doing up Hallowe'en complex-wide, complete with our own fireworks display and hot chocolate and marshmallows. Scaring the bejeebers out of the little ones, some people turned their units into dark, foggy caverns of spooky-dom. The kids wanted to go back every year, until it was no longer scary. In the complex, kids could fill their bags so heavy in no time at all. They could hardly carry them home.

Complex-wide garage sale days brought people out to meet each other and tut-tut over the junk we seem to amass. In such a tight environment, people could learn to work together very quickly and without much fuss. We had our own meeting room and would bring in fitness people, speakers, and music, organize sock-hops for older kids, hold craft sales or votes on repairing our old roofs.

A sense of community is an immediate product of living in an owner townhouse complex. I have heard that it is quite similar in a condo, an owner-apartment building. Some complexes fail to muster a community feeling, and it is usually because of the lack of imagination and energy to do things together, or a lack of common spaces like pools, playgrounds, or meeting rooms.

Children make it work more quickly. Children make you meet people. Most of us need a sense of community—of living *with* our neighbours, not just beside them. Your neighbours become people, with names and families and daily patterns that you come to know. Your lives entwine in a more immediate way than do most neighbours in single-family homes or apartment buildings: here, you meet on the street; you shovel snow side by side, your children play with their children, your house is open to them, you visit other parents where your children play.

One of the challenges with cheaper housing is that not many people stay very long. They "move up" to single-family homes, or more prestigious complexes, if they still like townhouse living. After all, you don't have to mow the lawns or prune the trees or paint the house or fix the roof. You just live there and take care of your place from the plaster in.

Maintaining a continuous sense of community is a challenge when some of the key people move on. This is where the institutions of your strata council can help keep the complex alive and friendly. Built into the organization can be everything from standing committees to organize annual events and programs to formal relationships with your city's parks and recreation department, to bring in leaders and programs using your facilities. This is becoming more common in my area. If a complex can retain a good name for itself, that history (and good documentation) often helps the new hands pick up where the others have left off. There may be ups and downs some years, but good visions and people keep a community alive.

On the whole, I'd say that townhouse complexes are probably enjoyed more by extroverts than introverts. It is hard to feel alone (or find solitude) surrounded by so much life. Many people enjoy that—need it, even. If you need a little more space and quiet or to make some noise or a mess, you move on.

The townhouse experience taught me a great deal about community living. With the right balance of personal and communal space, a basic set of rules to live by, and an organized life of events and participatory activities, you can achieve a strong sense of belonging and security. A true community is something we seem to need more of as we move about so often in search of work or a better lifestyle. It doesn't just happen. It seems you have to plan for it. Every home should be in an intentional community. It's really the intent that counts.

Maybe you have already heard of "intentional communities." I am just learning about a few new ones around British Columbia. There is also something called "co-housing," which I think is the same thing, only smaller. Some American developers have leapt onto the idea of recreating village life by building brand new ones. The concept is that by building a small community where everything is within walking distance and where everyone has front porches, people will automatically get to know all their neighbours and to enjoy living in a tight community. A developer's intention is to make money by building housing with the right "look." What makes a community is the right *people*.

Co-housing is an intentional community on the size of a townhouse development or condo unit, where the first buyers are the developers who design not only the physical structures but also the community life they choose to have. These people are choosing to frame their lives with their housing. Artists' communities build in workshops and galleries. Gardening communities build in gardens and compost heaps. Most build in community rooms and a list of social functions that keep everyone together. The intention is that people who think alike live supportively with one another. They want to put down roots with a web of likeminded people. It's more in the organizational intention of the group—saying *this is how we are going to live with one another*.

From what I have seen of townhouse and condo complexes in my area, an intentional culture can arise from within at any time, regardless of the original intentions of the first people who moved in. Co-op housing is similar. Some complexes are designed only for single-parent families, some for only single people or older people or for people with physical impairments.

I am also reminded of my year in residence at university. Residence is an intentional intellectual and social community. Students support each other. My college was named after Samuel de Champlain. In 1604, Champlain sailed to Acadia with the Sieur de Monts, who planned to establish a French colony there. Québec City later worked out better. Champlain had no position of command at either of the Acadian settlements at Ste-Croix or Port-Royal, but he is credited with creating "L'Ordre de Bon Temps" there, the Order of Good Cheer. During particularly harsh winters, a week-long (maybe month-long) roster of revelry and partying was instituted to break the winter doldrums of the men stationed there.

Of course, we followed his example at Champlain College. Teams entered snow sculpture contests or beer-swilling contests or poetry contests. Each to their own. Glad to dream up partying excuses, the tradition lives on among students hunkered down during long winter months in residences.

What seems to be happening today is that some people want to create a new kind of community living atmosphere where they can support each other and have fun with their lives. That was a model used by early settlers, almost always religious communities, where their faith and ideals kept them together as much as their sharing of the work.

The more things change, the more they remain the same. Townhouse communities can build that sense of community that we all need.

CHAPTER EIGHTEEN

Living in the Suburbs, Again

Eden Avenue, Coquitlam

All in all, I guess I had hoped we would never be living in a suburb. There are a few key things that happen in your life that make a suburb appealing. A major excuse is having children and having to think about the best place you'd like to raise them and still be able to find decent work for yourself, and probably your spouse, too. It depends on the kind of work you need, whether you can find it in small communities or only in larger ones. For me, more so than my wife, larger cities are the best places to find work. I had experience in post-secondary administration work and later in communications and public relations. Not much of that in the country, or even in small towns. My wife, the teacher, has a readily transportable career, but we often found that the most desirable small places were also full of teachers who wanted to live there, too. Jobs were scarce. Alas, though we really liked country living, we were strapped to city working.

You have to decide what sacrifices you are willing to make and what opportunities you are seeking for your children as well as for yourself. Suburbs have the advantages of being near cities and of generally having good schools, large enough to offer a wider range of programs than you might find at smaller schools in smaller communities. There are usually good recreation centres and libraries close by. You don't think you need such things that close to home when you are childless. Either the downtown life gets into your daily routine or, alternately, smaller even remote communities will do just fine. But add children, and everything changes.

You need room for a swing set or a playhouse. You need pets. You need more rooms. You need a garage to stow all the stuff that you accumulate. A single-family home in the suburbs seems like the obvious choice. It's not the country, but if you find a large lot in a quiet neighbourhood, you can imagine.

So, our next move was to the house we had in suburban Coquitlam, where I began writing this book. We had grown tired of the driving, the noise, and closeness of the townhouse complex we came from, and after eight years there, we were ready to move up to a single-family home.

When you know what you are looking for, with some experience behind you, as we had, you make your decisions fast. After looking in a chosen area for many months, I noticed a "For Sale" sign being hammered into the front lawn of a cute little white clapboard house. I approached the real estate salesman and asked the price. Then I asked him to put the sign back in his trunk. The next day, my wife and I toured the house and made a winning offer on the spot.

When we arrived back at our townhouse, the phone was ringing as I came in the door. It was a real estate agent asking us if we wanted to sell our old place, because he had buyers eager to get into the complex. They bought our townhouse the next morning. They, too, knew just what they wanted.

Two blocks from the library, seniors' centre, the swimming pool, recreation centre, ice rink and high school, our new location promised walking to everything and leaving the car to sit unpollutingly in the driveway. It was two blocks over to a small lake and park and four blocks over to a huge park that it took an hour and a half to walk around. And six or seven blocks to a small shopping plaza with all the basics—a grocery, drug store, bakery, bank, video store, restaurant, fast food spot, veterinary clinic, travel agency, dry cleaners, and a few others. Our new house had *location*! It was, however, the smallest, humblest house in the neighbourhood. Which meant it had a big yard—with fruit trees, a vegetable garden, and room to build a playhouse, which I did immediately.

This was the first house we had owned. It was a handful more than the townhouse, because every chore, every repair, and every improvement we would have to make ourselves. That's something you don't have when you rent: the ability to spend money endlessly on your own house. There's a saying that a boat is a hole in the water into which you pour money. A house is a hole in the ground into which you pour money. Some people only buy new houses, so they don't have to do that. I see the point.

Our thirty-five-year-old bungalow had lapped cedar siding painted white, with dark green shutters and trim. Almost a cottage, it had a quaint feel to it. In the front yard was a fully skirted Douglas fir tree stretching up some twenty-five metres. Douglas, as we called it, was like a friend. City work crews would take their lunch hour under it on a hot day. We often had a picnic lunch under it. James, our son, celebrated his stuffed animals' birthdays under it. Shading us in summer, cutting the wind in the fall, breaking the snowfalls of winter, and masking the houses on the far side of the street, Douglas had many jobs.

I continued my father's tradition of putting a recreation room in the basement with a warm brick fireplace and a gas fireplace insert. Flop-able foam sofa. Bins for toys. Open wooden slat shelving everywhere. Games piled high. Art supplies. Dress-up stuff. Toys. No bar. No attempts to be fancy for adults. Just really child friendly. In another basement room, my wife and I shared a large office space. When he was eight, our son moved downstairs to a bedroom beside the rec room. A new bathroom and laundry room were the last renovations we made.

Upstairs we had one bedroom, a TV room, a living and dining room, L-shaped, and a small kitchen and bathroom. When you move from smaller confines to a larger space, anything bigger seems better. Our cabin was forty-two square metres, and our townhouse, only one and a half times as large, on three levels, felt huge. This house was smallish by new home standards, only fifty square metres on each floor, but almost a third larger than the townhouse we had left.

In the backyard, we had a vegetable garden in one corner and the playhouse in the other, nestled between the large apple tree and the plum tree. At first, the kids played *in* the playhouse, but as they got older, they appeared to play more *on* it. Its interior was soon to be converted to a starship bridge deck or a time/space warp machine. That would be fitting. Coming out to the playhouse one spring for the first time in a while, our son found the kitchen setup too childish. The knights of the square plastic table took over. We adults play house with different houses. Children just reimagine the one they have.

It was great to have a garden again, even though it was the smallest we have ever had. Throughout the summer, almost everything on our dinner plate—except the meat or fish—came from the garden. Potatoes, tomatoes, beans, peas, corn, lettuce, and whatever else made it through the bugs and slugs. Our berries were purloined from bushes growing up and down the lanes in our neighbourhood, though some just grew over the fence into the lane. Some years we had to give away boxes of apples from our prolific tree. We ate fresh applesauce and apples well into winter. If we got to the plums before the raccoons did, we had a good feed of them, too. One year, we got there first and made freezer plum jam to enjoy later. Bag-loads of extra beans were secretly given to our neighbours. Those of you who grow your own know that there is nothing fresher-tasting or more flavourful than your own garden produce.

Our neighbourhood did not possess a true sense of community, though it was fairly neighbourly. We found that it took about three times as long in suburbia to create relationships with our neighbours as it did in the townhouse setting. Thirty-five years prior, this area had been field and bush, and then it became a suburb within the space of five years. Many of the original residents were still there, and it was they who provided the neighbourliness more than others. First of all, they knew each other very well. Their children went to school together. They'd seen each other's faces for over thirty years. When someone went away, the others watched over and tended to the vacant house. They'd help out if someone was sick or injured, bringing over meals or driving them to appointments.

My backyard neighbour, Frank, used to live in London, Ontario. That common ground between us produced several connections. One was a priest at an Anglican church in London that my mother attended. The same priest and rector of his church, Bruce Howe, and his mentor, Staf Tanton, had been influences in Frank's student life in Halifax in the 1950s. So, now my mother in London and my neighbour Frank were connected through the priest and me. That's what I mean by extensive relationships being more commonplace than family connections.

Buddy and Donna, in the house across the street, had lived there thirty-three years. Buddy retired early from the railway and leisurely took care of their house. Between buying and selling their condos and houses, their two grown and married children occasionally had to live there. Buddy and Donna liked that. Almost every weekend, the "kids" were back for a dinner or an afternoon. Our dog, Emmy, loved Buddy, too. Whenever he was out front, she'd sit on our side of the street and whine at him to come pay her a visit. Buddy lost his ten-year-old dog, a Shetland sheepdog, a few months back while on a walk. Some huge, vicious dog got loose and just chomped hard on it. There was nothing he could do. Emmy helped Buddy and Donna with their pain.

Ken and Norma, next door, were about the same age, also original inhabitants like Buddy and Donna. Norma was a retired teacher and Ken still worked much of the time as an electrician. Ken was husky and energetic and very talkative once you got him going. He'd tell you every detail of his day, interesting or not. But he was a wise old guy. His main contract was with the liquor control board, and he took care of most of their stores. Ken was especially talkative after doing the repairs on stores where thieves had driven a bulldozer or truck through the front windows and over the cash registers. He also got calls to re-wire houses that had been busted as pot-growing operations. I used to think an electrician's life would be boring.

As some of the original people moved out, the neighbourhood changed. When younger families like ours moved in, we'd have to start the community-building process over again. This time, it was built on different suppositions. First, the moms were not at home during the day, as most had been back in the sixties. Second, we seemed to have far less free time on our hands. People worked more, spent more hours being caught up in commuter traffic, and found more things to do outside the house and neighbourhood. Except in the summer, the back fence didn't get much conversation over it.

In some areas, there are strong community associations or neighbourhood associations that perform the function of greeters to newcomers. Someone knocks on your door, introduces you to your neighbours, invites you to meetings and parties, and tells you about programs for children and adults in the community. In unorganized areas, that doesn't happen. And it should. On streets like ours, if you don't really like or can't immediately appreciate the kind of neighbours who move in beside you, you're not tempted to strike up much of a relationship.

It is especially difficult when your new neighbours don't speak English, as so often happens in Canada's largest cities. In the Vancouver area, most new immigrants are from Asia, or occasionally from Eastern Europe or an Arab country. For the first year or two, you can't even communicate enough to tell them when to put their garbage out. They have come from a completely different world, and their expectations of neighbourliness and yours are often quite different. It is both difficult for you to fit them in and for them to fit *themselves* in. As Coquitlam's healthy communities coordinator at the time, I learned such things and helped start or restart neighbourhood associations. These associations also had the ear of city council in a more formal way and helped the city listen to community needs. That's what the project was all about.

Living in suburbia once again showed me that you needed some organization to make it work as a community and not just a place to live – to commute from. Sometimes that takes the form of a community association or simply a few go-getters who plan block parties or community dinners – whatever it takes.

In "The Last House" and the Epilogue I explore in more detail these kinds of challenges. What makes a healthy community and how does it happen?

CHAPTER NINETEEN

The Fabric House

Everyone raised in Canada knows the stories of the voyageurs: brave louts who paddled their canoes and camped their way from end to end of the vast untamed land. Behind them came the surveyors and explorers, who did much the same, and gave names to everything that was left. Following them were the true pioneers, those who tried to tame a piece of land—most, successfully. And we know of the Indigenous peoples who had little trouble, through much effort and knowledge, living in this great land, from north to south, east to west. All of them shine in our minds as resourceful and doggedly determined types who can survive all perils and rejoice in the joys and beauties of the natural state of the Canadian wilderness. For many adventurous Canadians, that heritage is often what propels us to take to our canoes and tents and to explore and commune with Canada's wilderness.

I have to consider my tent as a house, too. It qualifies. I calculate that I have lived in a tent for at least one year of my life so far. I guess I'd concede that it is more like a portable *room* than a portable *house*. Most of the time, it goes where real houses don't. Still, it feels like a house, which you come to know over time. My wife would agree.

It looks familiar in the distance. Its rustling, swishy sounds and its smell say "home." And it provides basic shelter. My parents camped a fair bit in large, smelly, canvas tourist tents. My wife and I started out with an orange Canadian Tire two-man backpacker, moved up to a blue tourister four-person, and then also had a more serious silver, six-person dome for campground camping. My son got to spend about a month of his summertime in a tent. Both my wife and I experienced the same in our childhoods.

Waking up in a hundred different places but in the same home, looking out the same door screen at new vistas and new mornings, we looked forward to camping every year. Our tent has been our home from the East Coast to the West Coast and to the depths of the Yukon. It has taken us to places that few human beings have ever seen, and it has saved our lives on windblown glaciers and opened out onto mystical mornings.

On the Chilkoot Trail, on the Alaska-Yukon border, there is a glaciated pass about midway on the four-day hike through rough mountain terrain. We were completing a segment of the travels of men and some notable ladies, to the Klondike gold rush on the Yukon River. Except we were doing this part backwards—carrying heavy packs down a steep mountain to ocean level. It was August 4, and we had been snowed upon.

My wife, Kate, began to do strange things as we made our way up a particularly obnoxious trail of loaf-sized, sharp-edged rock scree amid small torrents of icy runoff. She gave up stepping on high ground and stepping stones and just walked right through the water, soaking her boots. She didn't care. Keep going, she said.

We had only made it halfway to the next good campsite and it was already four o'clock. I could hear the bear bell jangling on her backpack. Usually, you walk smoothly enough that it doesn't dingle very often. As we emerged from the scree onto the edge of a mostly snow-covered plateau, Kate was really stumbling badly. I sensed what was wrong.

On a lumpy bare patch of alpine tundra, I quickly pitched the tent. Kate was no help. When I asked her to put the tent pole in at the other end, she couldn't figure out which end went up. It would have been perfectly obvious to someone who wasn't suffering mild hypothermia. The first sign is doing careless and stupid things, like if you were drunk.

After getting the stove up and running, I held her close in the sleeping bag, warmed the air in the tent with steam from the stove, and started getting warm soup and tea into her. (Breathing in warm, steamy air funnelled from the pot on the stove is said to be the best way to warm the body's core.) It took a while, but Kate was fine after a couple of hours.

It was time to survey exactly where we had camped—having had little choice about when and where to pitch our tent this time. About ten metres from the tent, I found a very well-worn and freshly used grizzly bears' trail. I returned to the tent and quickly hung up the bear bells. The dingling of the bells supposedly tells bears that humans are near, and they avoid you—or at least you don't surprise them. I hoped the bears understood the principles as well as I did.

Bear scat was everywhere. Looking around, I could see that this little area we camped in was like a mountain crossroads between four mountains and valleys. We were encamped somewhere near the four-way stop sign. I didn't feel up to moving us, and I don't think Kate would have benefited either. There was only one thing to do.

After drinking a great deal of tea, soup, and apple juice, I staked out a small but distinct territory around our campsite. I especially marked the place where I had buried our food and heaped rocks on top of it. And then we went to sleep with nothing between us and the grizzlies except a fragile fabric, two dingly bear bells, and a dozen squirts of pee. I am writing this story now, so you know it worked. Or at least no bears came by that evening.

There is a follow up to this saga. My clothes were soaked by morning. Rain that raced up the mountain face came at us sideways, up and under the tent fly and in through unusual places. We donned rain gear, and we set out through literally all kinds of weather. And obstacles. Apart from the house-sized boulders, we had to climb down all day to near Skagway. We were slowed most of all by a porcupine. He was trundling down the narrow path ahead of us, refusing to let us get by him. He simply led the way for an hour or more. Walking as fast as people is something that porcupines cannot do. They have kind of a slow sashay, and the top prickles rustle and sway from side to side.

At last, we came to a bit of a glen, with the path continuing a short distance on the other side. The porcupine positioned himself right at the mouth of the path and sat down. There being a log suitable for two to sit on in the glen, we decided to have something to eat and relax a bit and try to figure out the porcupine. It soon became apparent that we had been devilishly tricked. Porky was interested in lunch—ours! I bet hundreds of other hikers had fallen for this ruse, even though we all know you are not supposed to feed wildlife. When you encounter a critter who is used to human food and handouts, you have to think differently about that maxim. This porky may even have descended from a long line of expert moochers since the gold rush days.

Leaving some tasty morsels at the *other* side of the glen, Porky obligingly went to them, and we continued on our way at a brisk clip. My knees gave out near the end, and it was all I could do to keep moving. When we reached the trailhead, we called for a taxi from nearby Skagway, where we had one night to spend before boarding a ferry/cruise ship to Seattle. When the taxi driver picked us up, he explained that a hotel had burned down last winter and the rest were full, and so were half the houses in Skagway, which were trying to fill in with bed and breakfast offerings. They were all full. We sure didn't feel like camping again, but… Was there a campground near town?

At this point, the taxi driver says, "Let me talk to Goldie." On the crackling radio, we hear Goldie saying that yes, the hikers could come there. The deal was we could sleep on the dining room floor on foam pads, in our own sleeping bags. OK. How much? Five dollars. Each? No, for the two.

Goldie's place was an utterly drab, grey square box of a little house on the back streets of Skagway. Weeds grew up the fence around a postage-stamp-sized lawn with no gardens. It didn't look at all inviting, really. Except it looked not unlike some of the places we had lived in at one time. Inside, little plants and knickknacks and a general tidiness made it quaint.

Compared to our vision of lounging in a nice hotel, this was a bit of a letdown, but it would have to do. I couldn't walk another step. Goldie was friendly and matter of fact and even asked the taxi driver if he'd like a coffee before he went out again. It turned out that Goldie was the taxi driver's wife. He had never mentioned that. They were very cordial and quiet. We had a good sleep that night. Better than a hotel.

Another time, we awoke in our tent to find the world outside had changed completely from when we went to sleep. From a windy grit-in-your-teeth Saskatchewan night in May to being flattened to the ground with ten centimetres of wet snow on the tent the next morning. From the orange evening glow of a flowery alpine meadow with vistas of hundreds of kilometres to a morning of fog so dense you couldn't see your boots without bending over. Like being lost in cotton batten. Nothing was what it seemed.

The snow-flattening episode happened to us in the Qu'Appelle valley just east of Regina. A marvellous sight to behold after driving for two or three days across boring prairie, the valley is a deep gouge in the land with a lovely lake and river up the middle. Near one end is a campsite. It was completely deserted before the May long weekend, which was when we arrived. The brush hadn't been cleared, and the grass was long in every campsite, but we found one that would accommodate our tent.

You can't cook outside on a windy prairie day without getting grit in whatever you are cooking. The extra chewiness is not appreciated, but it does remind you of where you are. Icy gusts descended on us at dark, and we hunkered down in the tent for the night, still finding bits of grit in our mouths even after brushing our teeth, itself, evidently, a grit-attracting practice.

Whenever you camp in a new place, the sounds are different. Trees rustle with new sounds. The echoes of distant cars and trucks moan uniquely. Birds and the most surprising coyote howls leave your eyes wide open at times. What was that? Being the only campers, as we were there, sometimes you are given to wondering about weird locals or drifters that might be lurking about. Not that we've ever experienced any trouble camping in Canada—except for a few drunken parties.

So, off to sleep we went. As often happens in the cold of the middle of the night in a tent, I woke up and had to go pee. Usually, it's my wife, but this time, I awoke first. In the dimmest glimmer of morning, I could tell that it had been snowing a little. Venturing only a very few steps, I found my spot to do my thing. Peering into the void, I could have sworn I saw a pair of eyes move. I could have sworn I heard something move. *I swore.* Maybe a coyote, I thought. Nothing to worry about.

By morning, the tent was crushed to the ground. Almost a half metre of heavy snow had fallen silently after the wind had died down. We were awoken by having no room left above us to turn over in our sleeping bags. *For Pete's sake,* we cursed. As I unzipped the door, I again caught a glimpse of whatever animal it was darting into the snow and bushes. It wasn't a coyote. It was darker, and big enough to be a wolf. Were there wolves in these parts? I had no idea.

Cautiously, we crawled out and began digging out the tent and the cooking gear we had left out, now only a rough mound of snow. Burning up all this energy in the cold told us we needed a hearty Canadian breakfast. Out came the bacon and eggs and pancakes, the Coleman stove was fired up, and soon we ate twice as much as we thought we would. Then came company.

From out of the bushes, crouching low and carefully through the deep snow, came the beast of the night before. First came its black face with orange eyes, then the rest of its large black-and-white, blotchy body.

"Well, hello there," I tried to say nonchalantly. And then it scurried over to us and promptly flung itself on its back, legs akimbo. Mooch the pooch had arrived.

Somebody's farm dog, probably a German-shepherd/border-collie cross, had been keeping a watchful eye on us and breakfast. After feeding him the last tidbits of toast and bacon grease, he seemed very pleased with himself and sat at some distance as we packed up our camping gear. Sometime before we had finished, he silently slipped back into the bushes and was seen no more.

We later learned, with the French we knew, that Qu'Appelle means "Who calls?" Well, we had a ready answer for that, but the story behind the name was about a Cree brave who heard someone calling his name there. When he returned to his village, he found that his wife had died, and her last words had been calling out his name.

|||||||||||||||||||||||||||||||||||

Traveling along the Trans-Canada Highway leaving Thunder Bay for Winnipeg, we seemed to find the darndest little lakes. We enjoy a bit of snorkeling in interesting ponds, lakes, and rivers, and we had stopped to beat the heat of mid-day and go for a swim in a finger lake beside the road.

Swimming through long tendrils of lily-pad stems and other feathery water plants glowing in broken sunlight, we noticed that we couldn't get near the normally curious sunfish. Off they bolted, far ahead of us. Usually, they are fairly curious and hang around just out of reach. We continued on and I heard a yelp from Kate. Skulking not three metres from us was a gar fish as big as us. Its jaws seemed to be half the length of its thin body. Many, many teeth hung out the sides. One notices this. And its beady little eye.

While Kate, I think, actually walked on water to get out of there, I regained some composure to watch it swim murkily off into the weeds and reeds. I wasn't afraid after remembering the long jaw was only useful for catching maybe two or three sunfish at a snap charging into a school of them. It probably thought we were other gar fish. Or more tourists stopping by for a swim and a good scare.

Not far down the road, we decided to camp for the night beside another Canadian shield lake, but not to swim in it. We simply picked a rut leading off the road and followed it into a dark tunnel of tall trees, which quickly opened onto a little field of tall grass on a knoll overlooking the lake. It was a perfect little unmarked forestry campsite.

Kate had been reading a book by a health guru who had a suitable rural retreat for weight-loss New Agers in the Southern States. A friend of ours had visited this place and told us a bit about it. As she always does, Kate read until her eyes spun to put herself to sleep.

The next morning as we were waking up and listening to loud bird calls, Kate launched into this story recounting the vivid dreams she was having about this health spa she was reading about. She said the bird sounds were just like in her dream, and in her dream, she was walking down this tree-covered road with our friend and the guru and there where little rabbits hopping about everywhere. And the birds sounded the same. Really weird, she said.

I got dressed and unzipped the tent and looked out onto the grassy field.

"Shhh," I said. "Come here. You better have a look at this."

Kate came to the tent door and clasped her hands over her mouth. Her eyes bulged out of her head as she gasped and gasped, and sort of shrieked quietly.

"Just like in my dream! Just like in my dream! Those are the rabbits!"

Being totally unconcerned about our presence and Kate's dreams, a good dozen velveteen rabbits were slowly hopping about, eating sparkling dew-tipped shoots of clover. One guy sat about a metre in front of the tent and merely watched us as he munched. We watched them for a while through the screened window of the tent door, until we just had to go, you know. A few close rabbits moved off a bit as we headed into the bushes, but they didn't seem too bothered. They stayed for a while, all seemingly friendly, even when we had breakfast. Just like in Kate's dream.

By the time we had packed up, the rabbits were gone. Somehow, looking at the empty field of grass made us feel like maybe the rabbit thing had never happened. It was too surreal. There were no rabbits left. But as we drove out in the low early morning sun beaming shafts down the tree-covered road out to the highway, we found them gambolling in another patch of clover. Just like in Kate's dream.

||||||||||||||||||||||||||||||||

Many creatures have attacked our tent, which is something you don't often get with a house. The smallest was a gang of deer mice near Atlin, British Columbia, and near the Yukon border. These cute little guys made themselves right at home as soon as we arrived in the campsite. Kind of came running over to greet us. Sat rather nicely on the picnic table with their slightly large ears and feet. Only thumb-sized, they were nonetheless unafraid and waited for handouts. My wife discovered that they would even sit quietly in the palm of her hand to munch the crumbs. As soon as one was stuffed, there was another to take its place.

We were close to the Arctic Circle for the first time in our lives, and we stupidly sat around the campfire waiting for the sun to go down. Which it didn't. Sometime after midnight, it went behind a mountain and came out the other side on its way up again. It never did get dark. And we knew the mice would be trouble, so we put the food in the truck and went to bed.

A short time later, we were awoken by the strangest scraping and scratching noises. In the dim light of the night, we could see the silhouettes of a half-dozen little mice leaping a half metre up and onto the wall of our tent and then slowly sliding back to the ground. Over and over and over again. It was hard to say if they were trying to get in the tent for some reason or were just having a good time. We made sounds like dogs, and they finally gave up.

Camping a few years later, on the Pacific Ocean shore of Olympic National Park in Washington State, we ran into bigger problems. Or rather, they ran into us. Not just little deer mice this time, but full-sized deer. It seemed that the little glen we had chosen for our tent, which was just above the storm-washed logs at the high tideline, was a milling ground for deer waiting to go out onto the beaches to eat. There were no other clearings anywhere. And we had pitched the tent right in the middle of the trail to the beach. The deer were not happy about this.

First, the tent began to shake. Gently, then harder and harder. After checking with Kate, my youngest brother, and a friend, Don, who were with us on this hike, I found that none of us was doing the shaking. This scenario makes you think all kinds of things next. Of course, we tried simply ordering whatever or whoever to stop the shaking. Smart move, wouldn't you say? Well, it sort of worked for a while, and then there would be another tug or jerk. We got up the courage to look out.

Three or four deer were standing about, with one or two of them working over the guy lines from the tent, trying to pull them out of the ground. Indeed, as they moved away after seeing us and our flashlight, they tripped pathetically over the guy lines. In this national park, the deer have been protected for many generations, and they have little fear of humans. More like annoyance.

They really wanted us to move our tent off their path. More deer came silently ambling by some tripping over the lines. Others were more fortunate. Many bent down to tug at the guy lines. All of them ended up on the beach, perhaps a dozen or more, eating washed-up seaweed at low tide. They stayed until morning, and a few deer came back up the trail we were on, practically stepping over us while we ate breakfast. The others kept a respectable few metres away and circled around us. All mentioned with their eyes what bad form it was to camp in the middle of a deer trail. Humbly, we folded our tent and went on our way.

||||||||||||||||||||||||||||||||

The most ferocious tent-shaking we endured came from another source. On the way up the back roads to the Yukon with my wife, Kate, and a close friend of ours, John, we camped for the night in the heart of grizzly country. For two nights, we had avoided telling *bear stories*. When you are out in the wilderness, in bear country, you try not to tell stories that will keep you awake at night. We had joked about this, and now we felt we were ready to tell our bear stories.

Our friend was a native of the Yukon, and looked the part, with a longish beard and hair. He had traveled and worked in many remote areas before coming down with multiple sclerosis some years later. John was still sort of capable but was just a few months away from needing to be in a wheelchair. He got about on two canes or simply crawled on all fours. On hot days—and this was one of them—he was rendered weak and tired. The cool night air helped. After we had settled in for the night, cozy and snug in our sleeping bags, John took the first turn in storytelling.

He told us about an old Indigenous woman he once met who had been mauled by a grizzly. She had been living alone in a remote summer cabin and had gone berry-picking a few kilometres away. Unfortunately, the bear in the berry patch was not amused at her presence and tore into her. Bears don't often intend to kill you they just swat and rough you up to get you off their territory. Except people don't survive the experience as well as other bears do.

The tiny Indigenous woman was no match for the bear, as you might imagine, and she got torn up rather badly. Her left arm was broken and mangled up and her scalp was ripped off. Somehow, after the bear left, with her knowledge of medicinal plants and mud to soothe her wounds, she made it back to her cabin.

By herself, she set her broken arm and even stitched the gashes together. But what John remembered most of all was that, with only one hand, she had sewed her scalp back on. John told us that, and we believed him.

My own bear story was a little more personal. When I was a young Scout, maybe fourteen years old, our troop had a cabin on a creek on a ridge high above North Bay, Ontario, where I was living at the time. It was the middle of winter, and an older friend and I had been chosen to do the honours of going into the cabin the night before to get it ready for the rest of the troop coming for a sleepover the next morning.

Our parents, I'm sure with their hearts quaking, let us off Friday evening at the end of the road leading to the cabin. Stars shone brightly and twinkled on the very cold snow that lay deep and soft on the road. Clear, cold, and windless, there didn't seem to be anything to worry about. We donned our snowshoes and packs and set out on the two-kilometre trip to the cabin. There were a few farmhouses visible on the plowed main road, but they disappeared from our sight after a few minutes as we galumphed into the wilderness. Above us glittered a strip of a starry night, and on either side was thick forest. The snow wasn't quite so deep there, but still, you get tuckered quickly snowshoeing with a full pack on your back.

After not too long, we stopped to huff and puff. We heard our parents driving away for what seemed like forever. Sound carries so well in cold still air. We had to stop our heavy breathing to really hear well. Occasionally, we would hear a cracking or crackling sound somewhere in the distance, somewhere in the forest. We were not easily spooked, being hardy Scouts and all. Still, it would have been nice to know what was making those sounds. After some discussion, we decided it was just the cold snapping trees. Water gets into rotted and split sections, freezes, expands, and *crack*! The trunk or branch snaps open suddenly. Or maybe snow was slipping off branches. We'd seen it happen. On we went.

At our second huff-and-puff stop, we stopped for a smoke. Too young, and Scouts and all, I know; we were prepared, not perfect. As soon as we struck our matches to light up, we were riveted by the unmistakable glint of eyes in the dark, off in the forest maybe twenty metres away. We swore the best words we could think of. My friend fumbled in his pack for his flashlight and, finally producing it, pointed it at the forest. A dim glow emerged in front of us and quickly faded. Frozen batteries. More swearing. We lit other matches and held them high. Sure enough, every so often, there would be those eyes. First here, then there, then nothing.

We tried to think of what it might be. Maybe a cougar. Maybe a wolf or fox. Maybe a bear, but we doubted that; they'd be hibernating. Standing in the middle of the road didn't feel so good anymore, so we got underway again, with a plan. We walked side by side. Of course, with all this excitement, we soon had to stop again to catch our breath.

No doubt about it, we were now being followed. The eyes were back down the road, still twenty metres away. We decided it would be wise not to look weak or foolish. No tripping, and no more stopping. Of course, we did have to stop again, to catch our breath and see if we were still being followed. Yup.

This time, as we smoked another cigarette, we gathered kindling and got out whatever unnecessary paper we had with us. Just as we left, we lit a little fire in the middle of road and left it burning to try to throw off our followers. We had been closer to the cabin than we had thought, and we hurried up to it.

The key did nothing in the frozen lock. More matches, freezing fingers and threats of peeing on it finally thawed it and the door flew open. We jumped in.

Closing the door, we *yahoo*ed and *wahoo*ed for some time. Lighting the fireplace, the little barrel wood stove and the kerosene lamps made us feel safe and cozy. We both drifted off to sleep very quickly.

The next morning, we were busily melting snow on the stove and airing out the musty mattresses when the rest of the troop arrived. Noisy shouts went up. "They're here! They're OK!" Scouts and the troop leader were all smiles and really glad to see us.

"We thought you were goners!" one laughed.

Why?

Did we know we had been followed by a huge wolf pack—maybe twelve or fifteen in it? One wolf had the biggest paw prints you'd ever seen. Their tracks came onto our snowshoe tracks and practically obliterated them. Then the Scouts found little scraps of paper belonging to us and a place that looked like a real scuffle had taken place, and then the tracks were obscured by wolf tracks and… They were glad to find us alive and well.

But then, as the other Scouts clunked and clattered their way into the cabin, throwing their gear about, the *bear* hibernating under the cabin woke up. Noisily. Maybe like someone not too happy to have had his sleep disturbed. And letting us know it.

From under the cabin floor, too close to my feet to think about, a too-loud scratching and deep growls seeped upward, followed by a bumpy shaking of the whole cabin. Right under our feet! *We're all going to be torn apart!*

And right after that, it was so quiet you could hear a pin drop. A dozen Scouts had frozen in place, in fear, in terror. We waited, hearts pounding, for the next, the next... whatever was going to happen. Nothing happened, as it turned out. Waiting about five minutes in absolute silence, we were pretty sure the bear had gone back to sleep. The Scout leader took his boots off quietly and everyone followed suit. We tiptoed and whispered.

A brave soul ventured under the cabin a few hours later and found the bear curled up in the woodpile, having rearranged it to his liking. It seemed comatose so we elected to stay on anyway and practise being quiet. Which worked out, except for knowing that you were sleeping one bunk above a bear.

And the wolves?

Well, we knew that wolves don't attack people (unless the wolves are rabid, maybe), but they never let possible food out of their sight, either. Foolishly, we had behaved a little more like prey than predator the night before, and we decided to make up for it. Can't leave wolves with the wrong impression. This time we followed the wolves' trail quite a ways from camp and even peed out a bit of territory-marking on it. That ought to show them.

The bear was gone the next time we came to the cabin in the spring. And the next winter, four Scouts went in to open the cabin for winter camp. No bear. But it was good that we had practised being quiet. Skunks, that time.

||||||||||||||||||||||||||||||||

So, after telling these stories and a few others, we drifted off to sleep. Sometime in the night we thought we were goners for sure. Kate and

I awoke to the sounds of loud grunting and barking and moaning, and John, sitting bolt upright with arms outstretched, grabbing the tent sides and shaking the hell out of it. We dove back into our bags instantly, at first convinced that brave John was fending off a bear outside, all by himself. We weren't helping, as you may have noticed.

We called out to John, "What is it? What is it?" desperate to know what was going on and half asleep at once. We turned our flashlights on and looked around the tent—which was jumping and snapping about, with John still shaking it up.

John, we noticed, had his eyes closed. As we got his attention, his eyes opened, and we asked again and again, "What is it?"

After a few moments' reflection, he said, "Oh, never mind," lay down, and promptly went right back to sleep. Kate and I were left to deal with a certain quandary—wake him or not? We went back to sleep.

Some hours later, I saw that John's sleeping bag was empty. He probably had to go. In the dim dawn light, I looked all over for him and called out. No reply. No John. By this time, Kate was awake and joined the search. Come on, we thought, how far can a guy crawl in bush? He couldn't be far. Maybe a bear got him when he went out and dragged him off, we guessed. Maybe he had gotten lost. He was legally blind because of the MS, but he seemed able to see enough to get around. Except, perhaps, in the dark. We should try blowing the truck horn a few times. He'd surely hear that. Or a bear would.

When we opened the truck door, there was John, happily sleeping on the front bench seat. We chastised him up and down for scaring the pants off us like that. He said he didn't want to disturb us by coming back into the tent again, and anyway, the truck seat was comfortable.

John didn't mention a thing about his tent-shaking all morning, and we sort of forgot about it while we were packing up. It wasn't until we were all back in the truck and driving down the road that we asked him point blank what the hell had happened the night before. Now, when John laughs, the sound produced comes as much from his inhales as his exhales. This laugh took a long time to wind up to. He was amazed that what he thought was the last part of his dream was actually real.

"Well, I dreamed I was walking along the street in Kitsilano with a few friends and then I suddenly had this flash that you two were camping somewhere and there was a bear right outside your tent. I had to warn you about it, and I was frantically looking for a way to tell you. So finally, I found a phone booth and called you. The bear was getting closer and closer, and you wouldn't answer the phone. I was going crazy, shaking the phone booth, saying, 'Answer the damn phone,' over and over."

That's when we told him that we had woken him but that he wouldn't tell us why he was shaking the tent.

"Well, as soon as I saw you two in the tent, I realized that you wouldn't have a telephone to answer and that calling you was a stupid idea. I felt kind of foolish and didn't want to talk about it, so I just went back to sleep."

|||||||||||||||||||||||||||||||||

Another memory comes to mind of when I had camped with Scouts. I think this was the only other time I didn't camp in a tent. It was in the same area as the Scout cabin, near Duchene Creek, I think it was called. A few friends and I had decided to go winter camping once again, and we had chosen a small plateau a short hike on hunting skis above the Trans-Canada Highway. Hunting skis—at least that's what there were called—were about two metres long, rather wide, and had a cable binding that could be set to let your heal rise or clamped down for down-hilling. However, without a metal edge, they were no good for that, but they did make for passable jumping skis.

Very crisp, clear air hung still. The cold—and it was really cold—never bothered us. As soon as we had reached our goal, we were awestruck by the exceptionally clear night sky. No moon or city lights. Above us to the north, huge curtains of brightly coloured Northern Lights danced and crackled. Racing from one horizon to the other, up and down, shimmering in and out like a chorus line of harem dancers. We couldn't take our eyes off this magical sight. Whenever the lights dimmed out, the stars above and to the south shone so brightly we could see galaxies and nebulae. Above, the Milky Way was more than milky. It was like paste, so thick were the stars that it was like a white streak across the sky.

Before long, we gave up on the idea of setting up the tent, and instead we packed down a hollow in the snow, gathered a thick mat of evergreen boughs to cover it with, and laid out our sleeping bags and crawled in, clothes and all. We were not just sleeping under the stars but under the dazzling canopy of the universe.

After completing our quest, it wasn't the challenge I thought we could boast about. We didn't even take notice of the cold and snow, which were more friend than foe that night. Lying face up to the universe in all its splendour and glory and seeing nothing else as I drifted off to sleep, I felt I had become part of it. And you can't really talk to teenagers about stuff like that unless they had been there with you.

With our young son, James, we camped at Dinosaur Provincial Park in central Alberta. The campground is in the middle of the site where large numbers of dinosaurs, including T. Rex, were found. A moonscape of eroded rock and sand surrounds you. During our visit, we toured the Royal Tyrell Dinosaur Museum in nearby Drumheller. We took in a show about the earliest ocean life, from over five hundred million years ago, found in the Burgess Shales, somewhere in British Columbia. When we left Alberta, we toured Banff and pressed on down the road to any roadside campsite we could find near dinnertime.

We stopped to marvel at Kicking Horse Pass, where the railroad goes in and out of several spiral tunnels through the mountains that meet at the pass. Just a short jaunt down the road, within earshot of all the trains coming and going, was a roadside campground.

We were in Yoho National Park, where the amenities were few but adequate. It seemed fine, so we stopped and set up camp.

High above us on all sides were mountains and cliff faces. To the east, they shone a bright gold in the setting sun's light. In the shade, they brooded grey and black. Directly to the north of the campsite, hardly a hundred yards away, was a dark cliff with different-coloured layers to it. Up high, it was very dark, and it looked like miners had investigated long ago. There were holes and debris slides on it, though on such a sheer face, it seemed impossible to get up there.

After dinner, I wandered down a beaten path to read a large, stone marker I had seen from the road. I couldn't believe my eyes. This was the precise site of the Burgess Shales! Up high, on the cliff. This was also a World Heritage Site, as was Dinosaur Park. In both places, life teamed. It sprang forth from time ago, and somehow, we are all directly related to it. That is where we came from. A half-billion years of existence, right up there on the cliff. Around the campsite was shale debris, inside of which you could still find imprints of these early creatures.

And so, we slept together that cool night, our ancestors and us descendants. Roots. Really deep roots.

CHAPTER TWENTY

The Last House Chapter

Riverlane Estates, Port Coquitlam

I thought I had finished this book back in 1999, when we lived on Eden Avenue, and that I'd publish it at that time. My timing was really off as many publishers went under, and none were interested in one-book authors. For many authors, self-publishing is now rather easy.

It is 2025 (at this writing) and much has happened on the home front. By 2009, our son had grown up and moved out to his own apartment nearby. That left us, now retired from work, with a suburban house we no longer needed. Now what? That is a question that faces many people at our stage of life. We had the time and inclination to travel, and that meant finding a place where we wouldn't have to worry much about outdoor maintenance or about leaving it empty for longer periods. That left us with either a condo or a townhouse and the whole idea of strata ownership again.

You've heard that you can run into big problems with stratas, but there are also some that are well-run and maintained. Those are usually the more upscale ones, where money is not a big concern, and which are relatively new. So, we started looking. Storage issues for our canoe, our e-bikes, camping stuff, and my wife's big stash of music teaching supplies and resources (she planned on working part time for a while yet) soon eliminated the condos. Townhouses, then.

We greatly enjoy biking in nature as our principal daily exercise. There is a saying that "you should do the things you can't not do." So began a search in areas where you could open your garage door and go—be in nature and have lots of different rides. Eden Avenue was atop a big hill and there were only a couple of parks to ride in, so that area would not work. There was one city left in the Tri-Cities area, where we had now lived in two of the three. The third had three rivers—the Pitt, the Fraser, and the Coquitlam—and a great deal of flood plain, meadows, and fields, and still a few hills. But what it also had is bike (and walking) trails along all those rivers—and they were connected. We started looking—and riding in those areas.

To make a long search story short, we lucked out on a natural pond-side townhouse in a twelve-year-old complex two kilometres by back road to the Pitt River dyke trails. For us, it was perfect in every way. We sold Eden Avenue in five weeks—and that included a kitchen reno and much garden work! That was 2011. Fourteen years later, we're still here, and just as happy as the day we moved in.

Why? The theme of this book explains it well. It's a ninety-eight-unit complex, so there are close neighbours and a strong sense of community in our end. We have worked at that, though. We are, by nature, outgoing, curious about others, and chatty. In many ways, the townhouse community is cosmopolitan, like Montréal was (and is?), because few people live there all that long. We were all new, so establishing friendships was easy enough.

In our present townhouse complex, there's a mix of young families and older retired couples like us. There are two elementary schools within two blocks north and south, and a high school five blocks away. The complex borders on a nature park with large ponds and wide trails. Beyond that there's a golf course, with shopping plazas just within walking range if you are hale and hearty. It fits the "liveable city" description very nicely. This is a 96-percent-owner-occupied place. Yes, you could also rent in a complex like this.

In BC, where we live, 30 percent of people live in or own a condo/townhouse unit. That number is larger in metropolitan areas, and more than half of all construction these days is condos. We are creating concrete jungles again. Building community in towers is a challenge. And we need community.

A lot of people are spooked by the strata ownership idea. Yes, there are some bad examples out there, but also lots of good ones. And some stratas will have both good times and bad times. The good stratas have large savings accounts (contingency reserve funds—CRFs) because they have planned for the long-term replacements of major items like roofs, windows, siding, roadways, and so on. That means relatively large monthly contributions are banked—sometimes for decades before being spent. But it ideally prevents large sums being needed from owners when major upgrades happen. It also encourages much better ongoing maintenance and repairs to extend the life of a complex's major components. It attracts new owners who see the wisdom in spending adequately on ongoing maintenance as well as building the CRF. No worries. Or very few.

When we first moved in, we found ourselves near the beginning of the bank-account-building phase. The developers had originally established a monthly contribution that sounded nice but was not realistic, so up the levels went for the next decade. A large CRF is attractive to buyers and sellers alike—the ownership risks are reduced, and there is money to fix things should you need to do so fast. Yes, the monthly fees may be a bit higher than some, but you get what you pay for.

Another way to ensure your investment is to join the strata council that makes all these decisions. The larger the complex, the more people there will be to join. It is a volunteer effort, guided by the property management company you hire. Smaller stratas might be hard pressed to find those volunteers, and especially ones who have any experience needed or who can get along well with others and who understand how meetings work. Having a long management background, I decided to sign up a few years into our living here. After a few more years, I became president in 2017.

There has been a complete turnover in councillors since then, but the new ones have a variety of good skills and backgrounds, and they have remained on council now for several years and provide stability. Succession planning would be good, and one hopes that some current members will stay on council while new ones come aboard. But since it's not a hire-and-train company, planned succession is a bit more hit and miss. Same thing with your property management company. If there are too many changes there, history gets lost, maintenance schedules go sideways, future expectations are gone. Deep, abiding relationships are ideal.

You can run into differences among your members, too—a lot, or a little, if you are lucky. Spenders versus cheapskates, civilized people versus the not-so-nice, forward thinkers versus immediate-gratification types, new owners versus long-term owners, OCD types versus chill types, culture clashes. Most issues can be avoided by good and quick maintenance and repairs and no surprises. Money can be a problem in cheaper complexes but not so in upscale places. Further complicating things would be the number of owner-occupied vs rental units. Here, it is about 96 percent owner-occupied. Those are the realities. Smoothing out issues should be the property managers' job, if you've chosen a good one.

Building community means that people find ways to get to know each other, spend good times together, and bring new people into the fold. When COVID struck in March 2020, it looked like we'd all close our doors and stay inside for a while. My wife and I had music to keep us company. We are folk entertainers, called "The Other Will and Kate," or, when our son joins us on percussion, "Friendly Folk." I have run a local folk club here—Crossroads Coffeehouse—for many years. After hearing a new phenomenon start up—a few people banging pots and things nightly at 7 p.m. as a show of support for healthcare and frontline workers—we stuck our noses out, too, and banged along. It was good to see a few more neighbours every evening doing the same. We'd wave and ask, across the lane, how they were doing. Then we got an idea in the first week of April.

After the banging at 7 p.m., we'd set up a sound system in the middle of the lane, and from the front of our open garage, we'd sing out a few songs of comfort and resilience. The neighbours would happily hang out at a distance from each other, of course, and stick around and talk a for a while afterwards. It became a thing, and we did fifty concerts, ending on July first. It was quite remarkable, and the City of Port Coquitlam took notice.

We were not alone in doing this—many other musicians did the same in their neighbourhoods. Later came block parties where we set up our own dinners but mingled safely at a distance outside in the lane. We have been a friendlier community ever since.

CHAPTER TWENTY-ONE

Trailer Life

We did not expect that we'd get a travel trailer, but we did. In the swap between our last suburban home and our new townhome, we thought we'd have enough for a small yacht or a shared one from the proceeds. The "live aboard" idea came and went with a shortage of moorage spots close by and a shortage of boats that were of interest. Back to tenting, then. Well, wait a minute. We calculated that we had spent well over a year of our younger lives in a tent, and now, at our age, that was probably enough. How about a trailer, then? Glamping, I think tenters would call it.

We thought that "trailer people" were maybe not like tent campers. Not so rough and ready and not so… but maybe we were wrong to think we really knew.

There's a whole new pack of things to think about. Where to go with it? How long to be out there? Road trips or parking somewhere? How big? How small? How much money? Tow vehicle? OK, let's start there. We live in a townhouse now with an ordinary double garage. What fits in there that you can tow a trailer with? An SUV. Which one? What can it comfortably tow?

After a great deal of discussion, we came up with our short list of must-haves: a queen walk-around so we weren't climbing over each other; a full three-piece bathroom; a workable kitchen with a good-sized fridge and freezer because we eat fresh and cook most everything from scratch; enough storage for clothing and food and our musical instruments—a guitar, a couple of ukuleles—and our music. We would also need air conditioning that a Honda generator could run, but also solar power on the roof and big batteries for off-grid camping. Oh, and a plan to really use it and get our money's worth out of it. Let's be road-trippers. We've been coast to coast-to-coast camping, as you've learned. We came up with at least five summers' worth of long trips that would last two to three months each. That didn't even get to the idea of heading south for part of the winter. OK then, what fits for all of that?

Research turned up that a Volkswagen Touareg was rated to tow an impressive 7,700 pounds, but not a lot of hitch weight compared to a pickup. It would fit nicely in the garage, and we had owned several Volkswagens before. We settled on the TDI diesel version for more grunt and better mileage.

The trailer was another whole year of looking around, and the choices were many. Too small, too big, too heavy, too cheap and tacky, too dark inside, too long. When we finally made the choice, my wife thought that it was too big and long—that we should have been able to find something smaller. We didn't—we got a nineteen-foot Lance. Not big, not small, just right. This model had a convertible bed—– so that it had a living room with a sofa in the daytime and that folded down and a queen bed that folded out for a nice bedroom at night. It also had a slide-out that greatly opened up the space. We added the solar panels, batteries, and a backup generator just in case. We were ready.

So now, our summer lives were framed by this trailer and where it could go and what kind of life it could provide. The big difference between a trailer and a tent is that the former feels a bit more like a home. They can both go to many of the same places that are road accessible, but you can't backpack a trailer. You can decorate it a bit and it feels like a home. And yet you can take it all over the place!

You are probably asking whether we considered a motorhome. No, for the same money, you get a tow vehicle you can use all the time, and you can leave the trailer—the live-in part—behind. We greatly enjoy e-biking, as you know, so we had a big hitch installed on the trailer, and we can switch it back and forth to the Touareg. And off we go to find more bike trails.

Based out of the Metro Vancouver area, we made our first trip north to Alaska—all summer long. No rush, no big destination—the trip was the destination. The first thing you learn is that you can learn a lot from other travellers. They've already been to places you should visit! Chat people up. There is a certain camaraderie among road-trippers. Don't forget the local tourist bureaus—especially those staffed by locals. Just ask. So, we've been up north twice, across Canada once, and around BC and Vancouver Island four times. Mostly, we were out for two or three months at a time. We found you could even camp during COVID so long as you didn't travel too far. Campsites are generally very friendly places. Some travellers are now doing it all the time. It is called van life.

What we discovered was that we had a comfy little space in any weather to explore from. Apart from hitching up and unhitching, there was little to fuss about. At about 160 square feet, we could clean it up in ten minutes. We could entertain about four other people in the space, though just another couple was easier. There were much bigger trailers than ours, of course. But this one could fit in many natural parks that the big ones can't. So, if you like being outdoors and in provincial, state, and national parks, but not in a tent, this is for you. Yes, you can put a kid or two in it, too. Some models have a back bunk room.

We enjoyed staying in places for three days to two weeks or more, to really explore the surroundings—to hike or bike the trails and experience the area. Often, we would plan our travels around big music festivals, Indigenous festivals, and visiting friends we have from Whitehorse to Cape Breton Island. That all made being on the road for a couple of months well worthwhile. In the eight years we had the trailer, we spent 402 wonderful, adventurous, and comfy days in it. Spending time in nature is glorious, and being in a trailer makes it comfortable. This lifestyle is a great way to extend all the experiences of the fabric house, but with a roof. Yes, we often went to "the end of the road" and "the middle of nowhere"—two of our favourite places.

There is camping in parks and "transient" camping in trailer parks—or "RV resorts" for the fancier ones. Most trailer parks have a small number of open seasonal spots where you can rent for a day or two or a week or two. They bring in more revenue than the year-round monthly rental fees for a pad. Trailer park people come in a variety of types. There are "seasonals," where they only show up in summer (or in winter, down south), the full-timers (it's a place to live!), and workers at worker camps, where most of the extra spots are filled with seasonal road and construction workers, not tourists. Some are quite upscale, and some are not. Some have a great community spirit and neighbourliness and others not so much. Some are in prime tourist areas, and some are not. You learn as you go.

Would you like trailer park life? The newer "trailers" and mobile home parks are worth a look. No, you don't get much of a lot or space between your neighbours, but you are free from yard work and all that. Some people build small decks and put little gardens in, and voilà, you have a home. There is the financial side, too. If you can own your own pad (some places have that), then your pad and the mobile home on it can appreciate over time. Most others, though, will find trailer ownership and pad rental to be a depreciating cost, though the cost of rental would be much lower than a city apartment. Manufactured home parks are worth considering, but municipalities and developers seem slow to respond to the idea.

By our mid-seventies and in BC, finding the summer heat and forest fire season not to our liking, we sold the trailer. There are no fires on the ocean, so we will spend more of our summertime by and on the water or simply road-tripping by car on shorter notice. I do recommend travel trailer life. Or van life. Get out and go places.

FRAMED BY OUR HOUSES

Mark Twain famously said, "Travel is fatal to prejudice, bigotry, and narrow-mindedness, and many of our people need it sorely on these accounts." Indeed, you can't know your country until you have seen it from everywhere from its forests, fields, mountains, lakes, rivers, oceans, to its towns and cities. That takes quite a while: a whole life.

CHAPTER TWENTY-TWO

My Friends' Houses

I should say that I did not live in the next few houses I talk about. But I did stay in them long enough to learn that they had their own charms, or a "spirit of place" about them. I don't know where that expression comes from, but it usually refers to a landscape or region, not a single house. I think it should, sometimes.

When you visit an aboriginal person's house, as I have done from Ontario to the Northwest Territories, you often find it difficult to figure out who actually lives there. Because most reservations have an inadequate housing stock, too many people are forced to live in one house. A case in point was a week-long interview I had in Inuvik, NWT. The prospective job was as a communications director for Indigenous print, radio, and TV programs in the Western Arctic. The week-long interview was designed to really get to know the candidates. Part of the process was visiting people in their homes.

I would go to see someone and find the house full of people, who all sat in on our talks. More often than not, the person I went to see was living at a) his/her children's house, b) a parents' house, c) his sister's, d) his uncle's, f) his brother's, or g) a grandparent's house.

Wherever you went, the multi-generational, multi-sibling, multi-related family was present.

Inuvik homes, for the most part, are more practical and braver than pretty and spacious. Heating a home up there costs a small fortune, even with the oil and gas fields just offshore. Think about that silliness for a moment. Raised up on stilt-like foundations to keep the house's heat from melting the permafrost underneath, and to keep above the winter snows, the Inuvik house looks otherwise like a small, pre-built bungalow or rancher. There are other variations around town, of course, like log cabin styles. Anything that has a chance of surviving the Arctic elements is attempted.

Lawns and floral gardens are not part of the picture. On the ground, you find snowmobiles, gas and oil drums, children's bikes and trikes, and the huge-diameter metal pipes that transport water, sewage services, and electricity lines sway overhead to the homes. It is a far prettier sight in the winter snows, when it is also dark almost all the time, than it is in the summer. There are short periods in mid-summer when the Alaska poppies, lupine, and a bouquet of other flowers are in bloom. Some houses get a fresh coat of paint and order is given to things in the yard.

Inside a typical home, you do not notice much difference from homes in more southern places. There is the TV, sofas, chairs, carpets, dining room tables and the all the other usual furniture. It is the walls that are distinctive. The people here are Inuit, those who Americans still call "Eskimos."

Though they pass the winter mostly indoors, it is not where they want to be. Many people still maintain a winter trap line or fish through the ice. As soon as the weather breaks in the spring, many more "go out on the land" to fish, hunt, trap, and gather. Summer camps abound in all directions. A summer camp is simple—just a few sheds, perhaps, a place for a big cabin tent or small cabin and room for racks for drying, stretching, and hanging whatever can be trapped or caught.

The Mackenzie River delta lies all around Inuvik. To the west is Aklavik, a smaller town on a fork of the river, and to the north is

Tuktoyaktuk on the Arctic Ocean. Both are reached in winter by driving the ice highway—a snow-plowed strip down the frozen edge of the river. During break-up and freeze-up, you can't get to either place except by air.

A newly finished TV documentary I was shown told the story of a recent beluga whale hunt. The story took you from the prayerful and well-prepared start of taking a small boat into the ocean through the actual hunting and slaying to the neat and orderly carving-up of every morsel that is then divided among all the families participating. At these times, their lives are full of true excitement and achievement that "civilized" southerners will never glimpse.

Indigenous peoples live much like we used to a hundred and more years ago. They live with each other, work with each other, and share with each other. Think of our modern life in cities, where we work for people we don't know, with people we've never met before and with whom we share almost nothing anymore. The cultural gulf between Indigenous people and the rest of us is wide. Do we have something to teach them? To be more like us? Or should they be the teacher?

Indigenous people take great pride in their hunter-gatherer skills and accomplishments. To survive and thrive over millennia in this awesome, barren, cold and unforgiving Arctic shows the remarkable wits and perseverance these Northern people have. Surely, some of the skills they have are the same as those of our ancestors who managed to survive all the Ice Ages on Earth. We may pass our "more civilized" judgment on them for having to trap, hunt and kill to live on this land. But to them all, past and present, we owe our thanks for just being here.

I say all of this in order to explain what you see on the walls of their homes. Photographs of great hunting moments. People working with their hands. People dancing and drumming. The beat of life is loud here. There is at least one drum on every person's wall. Lithographs, a new technique applied to ancient Inuit artistic traditions and visions, adorn most walls. Stone carvings dot the windowsills and shelves. Rifles. Antler racks. The finery of their Indigenous clothing style.

Their walls are rich in who they are. They say who lives there. Like another face of the person you are looking at. I look around to see what my walls say about me.

I am both happy and sad to report that I did not get the job. I would have, except that the agency had mistakenly not advertised the job position in the North. After they did, it found a more suitable Indigenous person for the job. I was saved from ten months of night and cold, but not before my heart warmed greatly to these kind people whose walls tell rich stories that frame their lives.

|||||||||||||||||||||||||||||||||

Maritime houses, especially those built by shipbuilders, do not sit upon the land so much as they appear to dig themselves into it. I have spent some time in two such houses, one on each coast. On Tantallon Bay, south of Halifax, Nova Scotia, squats a two-century-old farmhouse. Part of the house is built into the gentle embankment it rests on. I think the builder must have designed it so that it could be as close to the ocean as possible—which was quite close.

The front door was of ten-centimetre squared oak beams braced together with thick iron bands and hinges as big as your forearm. A stone crib wall, maybe sixty centimetres thick at the bottom, rising to only thirty at the top, doubled as the foundation. Massive beams like the ribs of a ship crossed up and over the rooms. You could enjoy a good storm from inside, with the waves bashing against your front door. It's too bad they don't build houses like this on the American coasts where they get all the hurricanes. This house has laughed at several passing through.

On the Pacific Coast is the Rosario Resort, named after the Seattle shipbuilder who designed and constructed a mansion for himself in the San Yuan Islands between Seattle, Washington and Vancouver, British Columbia. In Rosario's house, you felt like you were above-deck rather than below it, as the Nova Scotia place felt. The same interior design features here were elegantly crafted of special woods imported from afar.

A flair for independent living in remote places could be found in both houses. Water came in, gravity-fed from a stream or artesian well above the house location. A small power plant was located uphill and out of earshot of the house. All the construction accounted for onslaughts from the sea or air. Nothing short of Armageddon would budge either one. Both homes will last centuries, as one already has.

Why don't we build more homes with the idea of them enduring all perils?

||||||||||||||||||||||||||||||||

Several homes that I visited were not occupied solely by humans, or just the usual pets like cats and dogs. In the late 1980s, I worked in the field of wildlife rehabilitation. Many of the special breed of people who care for injured and orphaned wildlife do so in their own homes. Instead of a lampshade, you have an owl perched there. Instead of a dresser full of clothes, it's full of baby birds. Instead of a backyard garden, you see pens for recovering birds or small mammals like skunks, opossums, and squirrels. Instead of a freezer full of people food, there are frozen rats and mice by the bag-load. You find other concoctions in the fridge, mealworms breeding in bread boxes, and other surprises. You watch where you step. Such houses are not for the faint of heart.

You enter such homes carefully. Birds of prey are just as territorial in a house as they are in the wild. If a male person comes to visit their mate (the rehabilitator), they will chase you out. If you are female, you can't wear jewellery, because even birds like shiny, pretty things. And so it goes.

One of the great advantages to having wildlife living with you is that you can learn so much about them, things that we need to know to provide the best level of care possible. Indeed, some of the really advanced care centres can provide far better care for wildlife than you will ever see humans getting in a hospital. Proper food is just one glaring example. Another is that they take the patients home with them, if necessary, to carry on twenty-four-hour care.

I must tell you that having wildlife living in your house is not something you want to do. First, there are very few wild animals that can survive the experience. It is also illegal unless you are a licensed wildlife rehabilitator. There are, however, a few individual cases where their injuries are not fixable, and euthanizing them seems too drastic. Some of these animals can be given to zoos or simply kept in cages, but that, too, can be overly cruel—and often overly expensive. There are a few of these individuals, however, that seem mellow enough to be able to be used as educational animals—going into schools or parks for shows about wildlife.

There is much debate among rehabilitators about how ethical this practice is. Some believe that it is kinder to allow an animal to die than to pen them up or keep them housebound their entire life. Others see it differently, but only with animals that do not seem to be stressed by their human treatment.

Animals large and small will bond with humans under special circumstances. Most often this occurs with very young animals seeing the human caregiver as its mother or parent. Geese are rather notorious for this. To avoid such bonding, wildlife rehabilitators now use puppets of their real parents for doing the care chores, or they use blinds, never letting them see the humans. When released, these animals will not be attracted to humans and can carry on their natural life in the wild.

I should tell you about a neighbour of mine who had worked for twenty years caring for wildlife. Most of the incoming patients wildlife rehabilitators see in the spring and early summer are babies whose nests or dens have been disturbed. Because providing the necessary twenty-four-hour care at the rehabilitation centre is not very practical, volunteers and staff take the little critters home with them at night. If you happen to drop by for a visit after dinner, you are usually handed a baby squirrel or a baby opossum or raccoon kit and a tiny bottle to feed it with. And then you get the warm, wet cloth to stimulate their little bowels with and clean up the attendant mess.

These are dedicated people, as you can see. This particular woman and her husband like the best part of the work, too—which is releasing the cured, mended or grown animals or birds back to the wild. One of my jobs at the Wildlife Rescue Association of BC was to tell these stories to our supporters in our newsletters. This is what the work of the volunteers, the supporters, and the staff is all about in the end. Here is one of those stories which was reprinted in our local newspaper, featuring my neighbours:

Blushing Birder Bares All
Two of our members, a husband and wife, had taken on the task of releasing a great blue heron. The bird had struck a wire and broken its leg. A vet had inserted a pin in the fracture, and the heron was ready to fly again in about six weeks. Our members took the bird to the marshes around Minnekada Park and hiked the dykes to a suitable location.

Carefully launching the gangly heron into the open sky, they watched it wing its way over the water.

The great blue heron alighted awkwardly on a small grassy hump poking up in the water some twenty yards out. Unfortunately, the water level was high and the clump of grass was not solid.

The heron scrambled to another and another before foolishly hanging on to the last mat of grass. The captain went down with the ship. Our members were mortified.

The heron was now soaked and struggling to swim—which they can do. The husband pulled off all his clothes—save his underwear—slithered down the embankment and into the mucky marsh.

He, too, tried the heron's tactic of leaping from clump to clump as each foothold sank. He made it to the heron alright, but the bird struck out at him repeatedly. His wife, though nearly collapsed from laughing, managed to call out that he would have to throw something over the heron's head to subdue it. He had only one thing on him that would do the trick at that particular moment. And so it was that the heron's head was festooned with men's underwear as the now naked ape again hopped from clump to clump with bird in arms.

It was difficult to be inconspicuous, but his wife was trying. It seemed to work. Man and bird were fine. They suspected that the heron had learned its lesson and left it to stand on terra firma to dry out. A few hours later, it moved off without incident.

Walking back to the parking lot, they exchanged sheepish glances with several other birders out that day, each of whom was carrying binoculars.

The houses of wildlife rehabilitators are not remarkable in any way except for the critters you find here and there. Often, people get into this field because of their love of animals, not because they have a lot of money. Usually, they live in less populated areas and have trouble raising enough money to build proper pens and cages, and so their house becomes the care centre. It just happens.

On my wife's side of the family, there was a distant relative, a solitary man whose job was as a track switcher in the Rocky Mountains 150 years ago. He lived in a small cabin beside the tracks and would come out to switch the tracks when he heard the train whistles coming his way. Somehow, he found an orphaned bear cub. Like all lonely men, he took to caring for it without realizing what was in store for him. It never left his side.

Not many details have survived to this day, but for many years, train-riders would hang out the windows shouting at the man that a bear was right behind him! How they lived together in that little cabin is anyone's guess, but they did. And neither was ever lonely again.

||||||||||||||||||||||||||||||||

I missed telling you about one house my family lived in in Toronto, or the suburb of Leaside, as it was known then. Between our move from London to North Bay, my father had to take some training in Toronto over the summer. Our belongings were packed away and we rented a furnished house on Don Lea Drive. The owners were away for a year, or possibly just the summer. I don't remember much about the house, except that it was white and had much better furniture than we could afford.

My recollections about staying there, at age twelve, were the pedestrian crossings on the busy street a block away where one lifted arm would instantly stop traffic in all directions. And at the Canadian National Exhibition, with its great rides and huge arcades, I blew every cent I had. Because it was summer, I did not meet other children or make any friends.

That house does have some significance for my wife, however. Her family lived just a few blocks away at the time. In my wife's class was Cathy Charney, the girl who lived in the house we rented that summer. Several times, my wife would be invited to lunch there. The family was Jewish and the only ones in the area, which was otherwise entirely wasp. They were interesting for being just a little different. If my wife hadn't had a summer cottage to be at, I might have met her eleven years earlier, knocking on the door to see if Cathy could come out to play.

|||||||||||||||||||||||||||||||||||

The connections to my wife, Kate, continue. When my parents moved to London, Ontario in 1974, they bought a house at the corner of Wortley Road and Briscoe Avenue. Across the street is Wortley Road Elementary School, where Kate's father went to school. His family home was only two houses down on the other side of Briscoe. My parents and Kate's father went to the same high school, London South, but Kate's father went about six years before my parents did. They had many of the same teachers.

I lived for a few months in my parents' house in 1975, while I was getting settled in London, finding a job and a house to live in. Kate was still finishing her last year at Laval University in Québec City, and it was out on strike, delaying her arrival until late the next summer. I found work at the University of Western Ontario, where Kate would go to do her Bachelor of Education, to become a teacher the year after that.

My parents' house was typical of south London homes: a two-storey, turn-of-the-century brick house with a front porch. My father's family home is two blocks away, and it is the same type and vintage. His sister still lived in it. Her house contained the family heirlooms from the Marshall side, but my parents' home had the Stevens' heirlooms and then some. And then a *lot more* some.

About the time I arrived in London, my mother had developed an interest in antiques. That interest soon festered into a passion. Even I got roped in and became "a buyer," that is, one who hunts for antique bargains at auctions and garage sales. My mother began her antique and collectible business the slow way, first setting up a table, then two or three at flea markets held on weekends. When that proved successful enough and the basement and garage of the house began to overfill, I talked her into going for it—renting a large downtown store.

Over the next few years, and my father retiring to help out, they did a good business. In the old building they started in, more shops opened up, and soon there was an emporium of antique stores in it. They eventually grew tired of working six and seven days a week, and of course, the landlord started to jack the rent to unworkable levels, so they gave it up.

Unfortunately, some of the best stock that had not sold made it back into the house, where much of it remained until my mother's passing.

With three sons and seven grandchildren who came to visit often, she kept two extra bedrooms upstairs, and much of the furniture and pictures still familiar to us. The house, though not of any significance in itself, was full of all our memories. Parents' homes are like that.

||||||||||||||||||||||||||||||||

One last place I lived in for a while that I did not tell you about earlier was our friend John's apartment in Vancouver, on Nootka Street. You may remember John of the bear stories in the "Fabric House" chapter. This was in the fall of 1980, and I had come to Vancouver to work and find a place to stay temporarily, until my wife finished her teaching contract to join me in January. John was up in the Yukon visiting his parents for most of the time, so I had the place to myself.

I felt a little uncomfortable there. It was not my kind of place, not my things, not my kind of life. And I looked out of place, too. The apartment building was entirely occupied by people with physical disabilities for whom it was specially built. My friend John was in a wheelchair, and he needed what this place offered: accessibility.

The wall switches were lower, the door handles huge, the taps "elephant ears," and so on. At either end of the building were winding ramp-ways, perfect for wheelchairs but a heck of long walk if you were mobile. For those who lived here, it was the best kind of home they could wish for.

The International Year of the Disabled was 1981, and this apartment was ahead of the game. It was a recognition that about one in twenty of us cannot make do in ordinary housing. Until this time, most people who needed to spend their waking hours in a wheelchair or with a walker had two choices: stay locked up in a house where others had to carry you in and out or live in the confines of an intermediate care centre, even if you weren't "sick." Only a few people could afford to modify, or better yet, build a house that was fully accessible.

We all take our independence for granted until we don't have it anymore. In a few years, I would be spending a great deal more time with people with even more severe disabilities than those who lived here. At Nootka, people were largely self-sufficient, needing little extra help with daily living. There were many others who longed for the day when their independence would come.

I worked for several years as an editor of a provincial newspaper for people with physical disabilities—*IMAGE*—published by the Kinsmen Rehabilitation Foundation of British Columbia. My job was to promote their worth and dignity and to point out the discrimination problems that these people faced. The foundation provided a great many living aids, wheelchairs, and other special equipment so that those who were disabled in some way could overcome their problems with the built-for-the-able-bodied world around them.

One group of people was hurting especially. They had no home, and it did not look like they ever would live in one again. They had all suffered severe spinal cord injuries and were quadriplegics, many breathing only with assistance from oxygen tubes or even portable "iron lungs" that compressed and decompressed their chests. All of them lived in special hospitals under intensive levels of care. All of them were homeless, dependent, and despondent about their future lives there. You cannot make a hospital bed a home, no matter how hard you try.

Many of these people had been in accidents, many of them not of their making or just of bad luck. Skiing accidents, falling on construction sites, or being the passenger in a vehicle driven by a drunk driver—like Rick Hansen. He was hitch-hiking and took a ride in the back of a pickup truck. You should remember Rick. I met him when he was dreaming his dream of wheel-chairing around the world. Foolishly, even I didn't think he could do it at first. But he was not the kind of guy who would take no for an answer. His Man in Motion World Tour lasted two years, but he made it. It helped other people dream, and to not take no for an answer.

In the early 1980s, much progress was being made in transferring technology to people who could really use it. The Kinsmen Rehabilitation Foundation was at the forefront of locating or engineering many new devices to help severely disabled people do some task. It would be my job to write the stories about the most severely disabled people living in hospital beds as they saw their dreams come true.

Four young men would be the trailblazers. Each was a quadriplegic. They operated new wheelchairs by sipping and puffing on a straw or tilting their heads, or by whatever means could be found to activate small switches that accomplished the given task. An apartment was to be specially built that would accommodate them. It would be located in the heart of Vancouver, close to a wonderful area called False Creek and the Granville Island Market, still the trendiest site in the province. All that was needed was a little ingenuity and engineering. That was accomplished, and they began their lives anew. Soon came the curb-cuts, the ramps, the lower switches, the automatically opening doors we see today.

More than all the technology that made this possible was something far more significant. It was their home in every way it should be. They made all the decisions about it. Decorating, furnishings, meal planning, scheduling. They would hire and fire, if so desired, their personal care attendants. They would decide what kind of care they needed, what kind of help they needed, if any, and what they would do with their own lives.

Most of them could still talk, of course, so they developed or found work that only required talking on the phone, like many able-bodied people do. And I remember seeing the figures that showed that the cost of "community care" was still lower than the cost of staying in a hospital bed. It still amazes me that so many people remain in hospital settings when it is the most foolish thing to do.

A short time after I began working for people with physical disabilities, I took on the plight of those with mental disabilities still living in institutions. My role was similar, writing their stories, but I also managed a local association that took on some of the work of relocating people from institutions to group homes. Again, working with their capacities, and often against society's biases and barriers, these people, too, saw their dreams come true—having a normal life, living in a house, doing their own thing.

I relate all of this to you because I want you to know that anyone—and I mean anyone—can live in a home of their own, be it an apartment or a house. If we care enough, it can be done.

EPILOGUE

I need to finish telling you about the changes in the neighbourhood where we currently live. I explained that some of the original residents have moved out, starting around the time we bought in some fourteen years ago. Many of the recent sales have been to new immigrants. Taiwanese, Hong Kong Chinese, East Indian, Arab, Japanese, Persian. When they first move in, many older ones cannot speak English well. Soon the children pick it up, but sometimes the parents remain difficult to communicate with. They all come with very different living experiences and expectations about living in a neighbourhood or community. Not only do we English Canadians have our own attitudes about various nationalities to cope with, but each of the immigrant groups often have attitude problems with each other and misunderstandings about us. Getting everyone together in a neighbourly way is going to take time.

It can take a while for we Canadian-born newcomers to enter into the neighbourly fold. It is doubly difficult for the new immigrants. Our region has experienced a very rapid influx of newcomers over a short time. That, more than anything, has made it all the more difficult for newcomers to fit into the Canadian suburban landscape and neighbourly culture. Unfortunately, most don't have much contact with their neighbours at first, but that changes.

Another part of that problem is that this neighbourhood did not have a plan or welcoming community group, nor did many other similar neighbourhoods in the area. For several years, I had worked part time as project coordinator of the City of Coquitlam Healthy Communities Project. I found other neighbourhoods expressing the same sentiments about newcomers. Existing neighbourhoods began to lose their neighbourliness. New ones never developed any sense of community, at least among the adults. The kids in schools just got on with it. Elementary schools acted as a blender. When my wife showed a group of K-1s a picture book of kids eating different meals from around the world, she asked them where they thought these children were from. "Canada!" they blurted out. That is their reality—they are fully at home with their diversity. They just hang out together and enjoy each other's company.

The newcomer adults do have community, however. By nationality, they group together among themselves in large extended family relationships, business relationships, and church relationships. Like anyone else, they need community. The difficult part for them is finding a sense of belonging and community with their Canadian neighbours, where we are most used to finding it. There is in Coquitlam an association that tries to do just that—helping build the bridges from within the Asian communities to those of us who have been here longer.

There is another group that tries to build links among the various Asian groups — Taiwanese, Hong Kong Chinese, Japanese, Vietnamese, and Korean—who seldom mingle with one another either. Political differences and history have much to do with that. Another factor is that those cultures have all been "closed societies," where outsiders had never had much of a welcome. I think that tourism has changed that in big ways.

Canada, multicultural place that it is, has had a different history. Our strength is in our diversity, our many skills and talents and tastes brought here from elsewhere, with all the business and cultural links that brings. We tend to see what we share in common rather than getting hung up on our differences. Teaching others how that operates, how it is good in the long run, is sometimes daunting. Our history with Asians is not particularly helpful. We had "head taxes" on Chinese workers in the early part of the twentieth century. The Canadian Chinese head tax was a racist policy that imposed a mandatory fee on only Chinese immigrants entering Canada, intended to restrict their immigration after their labour was no longer needed to build the Canadian Pacific Railway.

During the Second World War, we threw Canadian-born Japanese people into detention centres and seized their lands and businesses just to be sure. We denied them the right to vote until the 1950s. Our own racism lingers on in more subtle ways. How do you extend a welcome mat with a feeling of trust when these newcomers know our history? Still, we know the effort has to be made, however long it might take to be successful.

People in the neighbourhoods I was assigned to work in wanted to find ways of dealing with these challenges. The Healthy Communities task was to find ways of creating a community focus and finding people committed to bringing an organized community association into being for their neighbourhood. Two community associations grew out of that work. Both began work on making their areas more welcoming and involving for newcomers.

One of them is centred in a neighbourhood much like mine. The Burquitlam Community Association had a good chance of succeeding. Among its first directors was one English Canadian married to woman of Chinese ancestry, both of whom are heavily involved in the community. At the first round of director elections at the end of 1998, a well-spoken lawyer of Chinese descent topped the voting among a fairly white crowd. The association had much work to do, but I thought it would be successful. It started a community garden, and many people showed up and enjoyed gardening together and getting to know each other and their veggies! It was a good start.

The other community association was in a high-density, new area dotted with large apartment buildings and townhouse complexes. Almost everyone who lives there is new to the area, but they want to take charge of their community and direct how it grows and develops. By seizing on issues that affect everyone, the association provides common ground for all to come together. For its millennium party project, the association worked on bringing all the residents together in the local park for a big celebration.

It will take time to find ways of bringing very different people together, but I hope that one day every block has an official welcomer whose job it is to make all the introductions and to talk about life on the street and in the local neighbourhood. Maintaining a sense of community and friendly inclusion would be planned *and accomplished*.

In the course of my research, I did discover that neighbourhoods can do just that. Virtually across the street from one of the neighbourhoods I was working with, Burquitlam, is the subdivision called Glenayre, part of Port Moody. Construction started there in 1959. The builder and developer mapped out the entire neighbourhood and included, in its centre, a large park, a school and a church. The other thing he mapped out was a community association for the neighbourhood. Personally signing up every person who bought one of his new homes, he explained the importance and role that the association could play in their neighbourhood.

Sixty-seven years later, the Glenayre Community Association is as strong and vibrant as ever. Over 90 percent of the households are members. I remember that activities in the neighbourhood included Easter and Christmas parties for the children, a New Year's dinner and dance for the adults, and monthly meetings to address local issues and running their new community building. Twenty-five years ago, in partnership with the City of Port Moody, the association built a lovely little community centre that houses a preschool and a multi-purpose room for Cubs and Brownies, teen programs, and a host of other activities.

I was surprised to find this oasis of community life so close to the area in which I was working. Looking up the history of the area, I found that a strong sense of community had existed here before the 1950s, when the neighbourhood was built on the farmland that preceded the modern subdivisions. When it was farmland, there had been the proverbial little red schoolhouse on the main street and community life revolved around it. Like farming communities everywhere, people looked out for each other and worked together. When the subdivision-building began, no one on this side of the street thought to keep that spirit of community alive. Pity.

The lack of community we experience today in many areas is simply because someone hasn't given much thought to it. For early pioneering Canadians, all immigrants, it was the community of *work together or perish*. During our agrarian age, it was small villages and towns across the country where everyone knew everyone. Churches provided focus. Town halls provided meetings and dance space. Fairgrounds provided fun and excitement. Quilting bees. Barn raisings. Cattle drives. We worked together and lived together. Now we seem to work apart and live apart. And it is harder than ever to get together, because for so many of us, both partners work outside of our local community.

Today, many growing cities and districts do not focus on what it takes to actively create and maintain a healthy sense of community. Neighbourhoods are full of people who have little connection to one another. I am happy to say that there are many exceptions. Community associations or just darn good neighbours usually make it happen. My concern lies with helping those who don't have it.

How do we create community so that people do not become alienated? How can we provide them the support a big family would? How do we take care of each other? That is what community is all about, no matter where you live.

More importantly, whose job is it to get things moving? I would suggest that municipal governments have that responsibility, wherever they can dig up the money for doing it. You do need coordinators and neighbourhood newspapers and town hall meetings to get things moving. I have always found there are good people willing to take up the work once you give them the basic tools of organization, some general visions to aim for, and enough funding and support until they can stand on their own.

There have been lots of community organizations I should mention. Rotarians, Soroptimists, Lodges, Kinsmen, Elks, and so on. And sports teams and their organizations, are kept alive for children and adults alike.

I don't regret having moved around so much. I wouldn't be able to appreciate what being rooted truly means if I hadn't. I wouldn't be able to make a good choice in where to have a home. I intend to keep working on how to build a sense of community. No matter where you live, that is an essential ingredient to your happiness there.

||||||||||||||||||||||||||||||||

In this book, I have tried to include every house that I can remember living in. I counted any houses I stayed in for more than a few months. Otherwise, I would have to tell you about two boarding homes near Oshawa, one in Barrie, and a few dives that I flopped in on the way from here to there. I realize that you have to live in a place for some time to really get the feel of it, or for its smell to cling to your clothes.

Houses with character, charm, or history are easier to fall in love with than newer houses. New houses are just plain. Old houses have cupids and nymphs plastered into the bathroom ceiling. They have cubbies and narrow passageways between upstairs closets. They have spooky basements and interesting attics. They have stories to tell.

Wouldn't you appreciate seeing an effort in any new construction, to do something creative and beautiful, to make use of under-the-stairs spaces for kids to play, to create a real view of the outside, to build something memorable? I like cluster housing, where you have a close community on the street side and large backyards behind. I think every neighbourhood deserves to have at least a small community building and a park for all to use—lots of common-ground areas with lots of trees.

I don't think I'm the kind of person who would like to live in an apartment. For some of you apartment-dwellers, however, maybe there is a book in you about living in thirty different apartments.

I can't imagine what that would be like—so I might need to read your book.

The house where I lived was often far less significant than its location. A home, house, apartment, whatever, is your vantage point. What you can and cannot do in your local neighbourhood is determined by where your home is located. Finding the right house or apartment is not what I aim for anymore. I have learned that it is more important to choose your neighbourhood and the lifestyle you want first. Then find a home there.

Houses frame your life. I'm sure you've seen how that has been true for me. You may be able to more clearly see how your life has been similarly framed. I am now more confident in my choices of where I live and what kind of place I live in. Sometimes I worry that I will simply follow a known path to the next place, when that day comes. I remember that I used to enjoy playing in fields rather than following paths. There was so much more to discover. Maybe I will continue to wander a while, just to see what lies out there.

My advice might be...
Live beside somebody who has lived there a long time.
Have a field with a stream below it across the street.
Have a towering tree in your yard.
Grow your own food, and more than you need, so you can give some to your neighbours.
An ocean, a lake, or a pond is great to have just beyond your backyard.
Choose a house that has been lived in by others and keep it in its style.
Live close to a community centre and go there.
Get involved in your community life. It's there, even if you have to start it.
Have a friendly, cute dog to help you meet the neighbours.
Have children to help you get to know your neighbours.
Make your yard nice to look at, especially if your neighbours do.
Observe the local bylaws and rules in your strata if you live in one.
Observe the way your home frames your life.

WHERE THE AUTHOR HAS LIVED

For a few of the earlier places I lived in, I have no exact address and no pictures. For most of the others and all of the ones I owned, I do have original photos, and I found much more recent Google Maps pictures of them. At first, I wanted to see if the old homes were still there. I then noticed that *yes*, they were – and almost all had been carefully loved, kept, and updated. Those houses obviously had great meaning to those who did that work or inherited it from whoever fixed them up—to frame their lives.

1. Whetter Avenue, London, Ontario
2. Duchess Avenue, London, Ontario
3. Edward Avenue, London, Ontario
4. Baseline Road, London, Ontario
5. Ipperwash, Ontario
6. Beaufort Street, London, Ontario
7. Don Lea Drive, Leaside (Toronto), Ontario
8. Clarence Street, North Bay, Ontario
9. Cedar Drive, North Bay, Ontario
10. Lakeshore Drive, North Bay, Ontario
11. Roxboro, Québec – Where I boarded a few months

12. Dollard des Ormeaux, Québec
13. Barrie, Ontario – Where I boarded one summer, and lived in a house for a year
14. Minesing, Ontario
15. Trent University Residence, Peterborough, Ontario
16. Blue house – Reid St., Peterborough, Ontario
17. Parkhill, Peterborough, Ontario
18. Fleming Place, Peterborough, Ontario
19. Stewart Street, Peterborough, Ontario
20. Boulter, Ontario
21. Cottage at Paudash Lake, Ontario (near Bancroft)
22. St. Bernard, Québec
23. Whitby, Ontario – Where I boarded a few weeks
24. Stouffville, Ontario – Where I boarded a few weeks
25. Wortley Road, London, Ontario – My parents' home
26. Mt. Brydges, Ontario
27. John's apartment, Vancouver, British Columbia
28. Surrey, British Columbia
29. Brighton Beach, British Columbia
30. Easthill Townhouse, Port Moody, British Columbia
31. Eden Avenue, Coquitlam, British Columbia
32. Riverlane Estates, Port Coquitlam, British Columbia

Printed in Canada